THE
DIODE HANDBOOK

First Edition

Cletus J. Kaiser

*Published
by*

C J Publishing
398 Wintergrape Ln.
Rogersville, MO 65742

Table of Contents

Chapter 2   High-Voltage Rectifiers   39

Chapter 3   LEDs and OPTOs   55

Glossary

Acknowledgments

The author is thankful to The Lord.

The author is deeply indebted to his family and many friends for their continued support.

Preface

Since the completion of The Passive Trilogy, which consists of *The Capacitor Handbook*, *The Resistor Handbook*, and *The Inductor Handbook*, requests were made for information on the active components in the same type of reference handbook. This book provides guidance in using diodes in electronic and electrical circuits.

As with all of my books, the chapters are arranged with theory and construction information followed by application information. With all chapters arranged in this manner, reading and using this book for reference will be easier and faster.

Chapter 1

Diode Fundamentals

Semiconductor materials, such as germanium or silicon, are used for producing diodes. In their intrinsic (pure) crystalline form, they are poor conductors. But when an electro-static field is strong enough, any nonconductive material will ionize and valence electrons (electrons in the outermost layer of an atom) will be torn away from their atoms. This type of ion breakdown is called the *zener effect*.

Addition of an impurity, when growing or forming the semiconductor material crystal lattice under controlled laboratory conditions, is called doping. (Adding the proper impurity will determine either a negative-charged (N) or a positive-charged (P) crystal.) The N material has *extra* valence electrons. The P material *lacks* valence electrons which create holes. Arsenic doped germanium will produce N germanium. Gallium doped germanium will form P germanium. Phosphorus doped silicon will produce N silicon. Boron doped silicon will produce P silicon.

Intrinsic germanium and silicon are poor conductors at low temperatures; but when doped and at room temperatures, they are relatively good conductors for electron current flow. When normally doped, silicon has about one thousand times the resistance value than germanium. Power diodes are usually of silicon because silicon withstands heat better than germanium.

A diode consists of a single PN junction. This junction is formed when "P" semiconductor crystal is either fused or grown together during crystallization with "N" semiconductor crystal. The diode has three areas: the N section, the P section, and the zero-charged (neutral) junction or barrier. At the junction, a barrier field is created by the combining of positive holes and negative free electrons from the two dissimilar adjacent semiconductor materials. The junction barrier represents a threshold voltage level that must be exceeded in order to make current flow. The barrier takes an applied voltage (almost 0.7V for silicon or about 0.3V for germanium) before the barrier disappears and the diode conducts or is turned "ON."

PN Junction

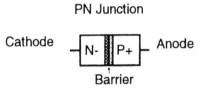

Two common techniques for fabricating PN junctions are planar and deep-diffused. Severe angles are often present on a deep-diffused junction, creating a "mesa" appearance. Also, epitaxially-grown silicon may be used in either technique and a variety of dopants can be used. Many variations of each technique exist from one manufacturer to another.

Polarity marking on a diode package may consist of a single contrasting color band or a minimum of three contrasting color dots spaced around the periphery of the cathode end.

Diode schematic symbol and polarity marking.

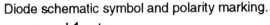

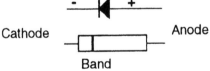

Basic theory of operation
Semiconductor diodes have a single PN junction and are a two-terminal solid-state device having an anode (+) and a cathode (-) terminal. The diode has a characteristic of allowing current to flow in only one direction. Forward current flows from anode to cathode (direction of arrow).

Semiconductor diodes have a nonlinear voltage-current operating curve. Diodes have asymmetrical voltage-current operating characteristics.

Voltage-Current (V-I) Curve for a silicon junction diode.

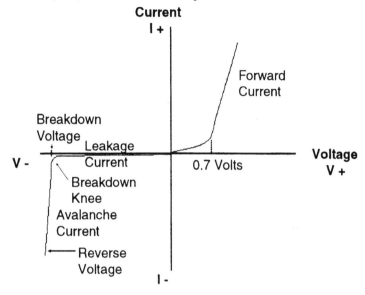

In the forward characteristic of the V-I curve, the semiconductor diode will conduct a small amount of current in the forward direction up to a threshold voltage. After that voltage is exceeded, the diode conducts and then forward current flows. The forward voltage drop is specified at a forward current.

In the reverse characteristic of the V-I curve, there is some leakage current up until the reverse breakdown voltage is reached. This leakage is undesirable; the lower the better. Leakage current is specified at a voltage less then the breakdown voltage. The diode has an avalanche effect at the breakdown voltage.

As the reverse voltage increases, the leakage current remains essentially constant until the breakdown voltage is reached. The current then increases dramatically. This breakdown voltage is the zener voltage for zener diodes. For the conventional diode it is imperative to operate below this breakdown voltage, while the zener diode is intended to operate at that voltage. Thus, the zener diode finds its greatest application used as a voltage regulator.

The current rating of a diode is determined primarily by the size of the diode chip, the package material, and the configuration of the package. Average current rating is used, *not* RMS current. A larger chip and package of high thermal conductivity are both conducive of a higher current rating.

The switching speed of a diode depends upon its construction and fabrication. In general, the smaller the chip the faster it switches, with other things being equal. The chip geometry, doping levels, and the temperature during growth determines switching speeds. The reverse recovery time, (t_{rr}), is the time it takes the diode to switch from "ON" to "OFF" and is usually the limiting operating electrical parameter.

The term diode and rectifier can be used interchangeably. A diode usually refers to a small signal device with current typically in the milli-amp range. A rectifier is a power device conducting from 1 to 1000 amps or more.

Diode Biasing

When the positive side of a DC power source is connected to the P region and the negative side to the N region, the junction barrier disappears. Current flows through the semiconductor. The junction, or diode, is *forward-biased*. When the diode is forward-biased (anode positive with respect to cathode), its forward current $(I = I_F)$ increases rapidly with increasing voltage. That is, the resistance becomes very low.

In germanium diodes, about 0.3V of forward bias may be required to start current flow, whereas, silicon diodes require almost 0.7V of forward bias before current begins to pass.

Reversing the polarity of the DC power source results in pulling holes and electrons apart at the junction, thus widening the junction barrier area. The junction, or diode, is *reversed-biased*, and no current should be flowing through it. When the diode is reversed-biased (anode negative with respect to cathode), its reverse current $(-I = I_R)$ is extremely low. This is only valid until the breakdown voltage, $V_{(BR)}$, has been reached. When the reverse voltage is slightly higher than the breakdown voltage, a sharp rise in reverse current results.

Diode Fundamentals

When the DC power source is replaced with an AC power source, during half of each AC cycle a current would flow. During the other half AC cycle, no current would flow. The diode rectifies (to make unidirectional) the AC and thus pulsating DC is produced.

When sufficient reverse bias is applied, a point will be reached where the crystal lattice breaks down and high current may flow in the reverse direction. This avalanche effect may destroy the junction and the device if the current is allowed to become excessive. The voltage at which avalanche starts is commonly known as the zener voltage. The operation of zener diodes use this principle. Zener diodes are special reversed-biased silicon diodes which result from a specified applied reverse voltage onward in a rapid increase of reverse current avalanche or zener breakdown volage. Due to the sharp rise of the reverse current, the corresponding breakdown voltage is nearly constant. Zener diodes can be used as voltage regulator diodes which develops an essentially constant voltage across its terminals throughout a specified current range.

When a diode is reversed-biased, the barrier acts as a dielectric and the diode acts as a capacitor. When the reverse voltage is increased, the barrier widens and the capacitance value decreases. In an LC (inductance-capacitance) circuit, the resonant frequency can be controlled when a reversed-biased diode is connected across it and the bias voltage is varied. The diode must be in a reversed-biased state constantly. This is a typical application of the theory of the junction diode when a diode is used as a voltage-controlled capacitor (varactor). Reversed-biasing has its advantages.

REVERSE BREAKDOWN VOLTAGE ($V_{(BR)}$)
Semiconductors have practical reverse-voltage limitations. The reverse breakdown voltage of silicon is determined primarily by three factors:

- the resistivity of the silicon (avalanche),
- the depletion region width (punch-through or reach-through),
- and the surface stress at the junction/passivation (zener) interface.

Reverse breakdown occurs when the voltage stress across one of these three areas exceeds the withstanding threshold and throws a high reverse current across the entire junction area. This condition is nondestructive in properly designed devices, provided that the reverse current is limited to a level that minimizes thermal dissipation. This phenomenon should be seen as "water flowing over a spillway" and not as a failure of dielectric material, which is a catastrophic condition.

REVERSE VOLTAGE AND THE DEPLETION REGION

The depletion region increases in the direction of the weakest field (the area of highest resistivity) as reverse voltage is applied. This expansion continues as the reverse voltage is increased until the stress on the field reaches the breakdown threshold. Epitaxially-grown layers have very abrupt differences in resistivity layers while deep-diffused devices are less abrupt.

Zener diodes routinely operate in the voltage breakdown mode and are designed for breakdown to be initiated by resistivity limitations rather than punch-through or avalanche. It should be noted, however, that high voltage zener diodes are less practical because the higher-resistivity silicon and deeper diffusion depths required to achieve the higher voltage ratings make it difficult to predict the voltage at which breakdown occurs.

Three nondestructive breakdown mechanisms are listed below:

Breakdown By	Descriptive Term
depletion region	punch-through or reach-through
junction/passivation interface	avalanche
resistivity	zener

Rectifiers are generally subjected to a peak inverse voltage (PIV) test to characterize their breakdown characteristics. This test is performed by applying 60-hertz half-wave reverse voltage of sufficient amplitude to initiate breakdown. During the test, the reverse current is usually limited to 50 micro-amps. The resulting waveform is observed on a oscilloscope to determine the sharpness of the "knee" at the point of breakdown. Both planar and deep-diffusion processes yield controlled avalanches under PIV test conditions.

Electrical Operating Specifications

The following operating conditions of Peak Inverse Voltage, Reverse Leakage Current, Reverse Recovery Time, and Forward Voltage Drop will now be discussed in detail.

PEAK INVERSE VOLTAGE (PIV)

PIV rating is the maximum reverse voltage (or the avalanche point) that a diode will be capable of blocking. PIV must never be exceeded in any application condition (unless specific controlled conditions are agreed upon). The PIV rating is normally specified by the manufacturer at a certain temperature and at the absolute worse case reverse voltage.

The PIV test consists of applying rectified 60Hz reverse voltage sufficient to avalanche the diode while controlling reverse current. Test criteria for diodes are established by the manufacture and these parameters are stated on the specification data sheet for the device.

REVERSE LEAKAGE CURRENT (I_R)

Reverse leakage is the amount of current that flows back through the silicon junction while reverse voltage bias is applied. The greatest influence on I_R is usually junction temperature, (T_j). I_R vs. T_j graphs are available on most diode specification sheets. Reverse leakage also occurs in the dielectric material surrounding the silicon junction but is usually negligible in properly constructed devices. A common approximation is to assume that I_R doubles every 10°C.

The following chart lists major influences on reverse leakage:

	Effect on I_R	Linear	Nonlinear
Junction Temperature	T_j increases I_R increases		X
Reverse Recovery Time	t_{rr} increases I_R decreases		X
Reverse Voltage	V_R increases I_R increases	X	

I_R rating is the maximum reverse leakage current allowed at specific reverse voltage and temperature conditions. Two I_R ratings are normally specified:
- I_R at PIV at 25°C.
- I_R at PIV at elevated temperature (normally 100°C or 150°C).

Reverse current flows through the diode junction when reverse voltage is applied. Factors influencing the amplitude of the reverse current include:
- Dopants used
- Junction temperature
- Thickness of the silicon
- Exposure of the junction to light
- Amplitude of the reverse voltage
- Cross-sectional area of the junction
- Amount of radiation impinging on the junction.

REVERSE RECOVERY LOSSES

Reverse recovery losses are a function of stored charge in the silicon junction and result in reverse current flowing through the junction during the transition from forward conduction mode to reverse blocking mode. As circuit switching speeds become faster, decreased reverse recovery times are required. Reverse recovery time, (t_{rr}), is the time it takes a diode to switch from ON to OFF. This time is shortened by many methods, all of which result in increased forward voltage and reverse current. The diode still conducts after the signal reverses. This delay time must be taken into consideration, otherwise the diode overheats as the efficiency of the diode deteriorates and finally the failure of the diode.

The t_{rr} rating is the maximum time required to achieve reverse blocking after a diode has been in the forward current conduction mode. Variations in test equipment and test sensitivity to lead inductance result in test data correlation difficulties. The t_{rr} varies with temperature, forward current, and reverse current. Normal ratings specified by the manufacturer have the testing conditions stated on the specification data sheet for the device.

The following chart lists major influences on Reverse Recovery Losses:

	Effect on t_{rr}	Linear	Nonlinear
Diode Peak Reverse Voltage	PIV increases t_{rr} increases		X
Temperature Junction	T_j increases t_{rr} increases	X	

Reverse recovery time (t_{rr}) varies with:
- Resistivity
- Temperature
- Junction width
- Type of dopant
- Forward current
- Dopant concentration
- Change in reverse current with time (dI/dT).

Circuit Effects

The slope of Reverse Current with Time (dI/dT) -

In general, t_{rr} decreases as dI/dT increases. Rate of change varies with manufacturing process and speed of the device. Typically, slower devices exhibit less change in t_{rr} as dI/dT changes. Waveforms are on data sheet.

Environmental Effects

Junction Temperature (Tj) -

In general, t_{rr} increases with junction temperature. Rate of change varies with manufacturing process and speed of the device. Higher speed devices of the same manufacturing process change more with temperature than slower devices.

Silicon Resistivity

In general, t_{rr} increases as silicon resistivity increases. The primary factor is the level of doping during the silicon ingot growing process. (Subsequent doping at the wafer level may yield greater variations in t_{rr} than during ingot manufacturing.)

Peak Inverse Voltage (PIV)

In general, t_{rr} increases as PIV increases. The primary factor is the high resistivity of starting material.

Manufacturing Process

Many processes are used to manufacture high speed devices (e.g., platinum doping, gold doping, irradiation, etc.). Each process results in somewhat different diode behavior.

Rule of thumb: NOTE: t_{rr} requirements listed below may be inadequate for extremely square waves or waves that exhibit significant ringing.

Input Frequency	Input Voltage Waveform	t_{rr} (Max.) Required
0-2KHz	Sine	2μS
2KHz to 25KHz	Sine	200nS
25KHz to 50KHz	Sine	100nS
50KHz to 100KHz	Sine	70nS
0-1 KHz	Square	2μS
1KHz to 10KHz	Square	200nS
10KHz to 25KHz	Square	100nS
25KHz to 50KHz	Square	70nS

FORWARD VOLTAGE (V_F)

Forward Voltage is the amount of voltage drop that occurs in silicon and is primarily a function of silicon resistivity. The greatest influence on forward voltage (V_F) is forward current (I_F). V_F vs. I_F graphs are available on most diode specification sheets.

V_F rating is maximum forward voltage at specific forward current and temperature conditions. Normal rating specified:
- V_F at I_F at 25°C.

The following chart lists major influences on forward voltage:

	Effect on V_F	Linear	Nonlinear
Forward Current	I_F increases V_F increases		X
Diode Peak Inverse Voltage	PIV increases V_F increases		X
Junction Temperature	T_j increases V_F decreases	X	
Reverse Recovery Time	t_{rr} increases V_F decreases		X

Forward voltage varies with:
- Resistivity
- Temperature
- Current density
- Type of dopant
- Thickness of silicon
- Level of dopant concentration.

PULSE POWER RATING

The admissible dissipation of diodes, rectifiers, and zener diodes which operate from sinusoidal supplies is based on the arithmetic mean of junction temperature and power dissipation. Devices which handle pulses are capable of passing short-term currents far in excess of the maximum admissible static dissipation. In this case, it is admissible to exceed the continuous dissipation curve for the duration of each pulse. The magnitude of the admissible current is then inversely proportional to the pulse duty factor, because power is dissipated only intermittently, and the thermal capacity of the system and heat conduction prevent an undue rise in junction temperature. Some of the data sheets contain diagrams which allow the rating of a device operating under pulsed conditions.

CURRENT SURGE

Current surges may occur at supply turn-on, turn-off, or as a repetitive condition in the operation of a diode. The specification must reflect a realistic approximation of the known or suspected condition. The effect of a current surge is a fast thermal shock which normally introduces severe mechanical stress on the silicon die and the surrounding package. The result can be a permanent degradation of the diode if inadequately designed.

Surge current is normally specified at a certain temperature for one cycle with a stated duration.

Rule of thumb: Current surge approximations can be interpolated from specified surge currents by using I^2t relationship as a maximum.

THERMAL IMPEDANCE

Thermal impedance quantifies the efficiency of heat transfer from silicon junction(s) to an external heat sink (i.e., air, aluminum, PC board, etc.). Thermal impedance must be calculated for each diode as well as an entire diode assembly. Proper understanding of heat transfer is a major key to successful diode assembly design.

DIELECTRIC INSULATION

Dielectric insulation is the material that is used for internal encapsulation of rectifier assemblies as well as the material that surrounds an encapsulated assembly. Heat dissipation, environmental conditions, weight, size, and external factors must be considered in selecting an appropriate dielectic material.

HEAT DISSIPATION

Many materials that have excellent dielectric strength characteristics are poor thermal conductors (i.e., most silicone rubbers) and are mostly unsuitable for rectifier assemblies that dissipate more that one watt.

CORONA

Corona is the result of ionization of gas (air, oxygen, etc.) that is caused by a high-voltage field. This extremely destructive phenomenon usually results in slow degradation of insulating materials that can result in hidden or potential failures. Careful design, consistent manufacturing processes, eliminating air entrapment in encapsulation, and thorough understanding of causes of corona are required to minimize this problem.

ENVIRONMENTAL CONDITIONS

Many materials that have excellent dielectric characteristics have qualities that are unacceptable in certain environments. Consider the following:

Humidity

Humid environments may result in moisture absorption in the dielectric materials or severely limit voltage ratings in air-insulated applications. Air insulation of 10KV/inch (min.) is the rule of thumb in normal environments. High humidity may require hermetic sealing or encapsulation of exposed electrical conductors or connectors.

High Temperature

High temperature may severely reduce the voltage rating of some dielectric materials or induce mechanical stress due to mismatched thermal expansion coefficients. Materials may also degrade significantly at high temperature.

Consider the following:

Temperature Range	Material Availability
+25°C to +75°C	Excellent
+75°C to +125°C	Good
+125°C to +175°C	Fair
+175°C to +225°C	Poor
> +225°C	Rare

Low Temperature

Low temperature primarily presents mechanical stress problems. Many materials become brittle, fragile, or shrink nonlinearly at very low temperatures. Consider the following:

Temperature Range	Material Availability
- 40°C to +25°C	Excellent
- 55°C to - 40°C	Good
- 65°C to - 55°C	Fair
< - 65°C	Rare

High Altitude

High altitude presents numerous problems. Corona problems will vary nonlinearly with altitude. The cooling in space is limited primarily to thermal radiation. Certain materials outgas in space and may degrade or deposit films of insulation on connectors and components. High altitude applications require detail analysis of all factors.

Chemical

Insulating oil is commonly used in applications >50KV and significantly reduces mechanical stress, corona, and air void problems when compared with solid encapsulation. However, some dielectric fluids may remove labels, swell encapsulants, degrade encapsulants, or cause other damage. Careful consideration must be given to material compatibilities in applications that utilize liquid dielectrics.

Soldering Components

A. Wave soldering has the highest solder temperature and heat transfer rates that are imposed on small resin molded parts like transistors, integrated circuits, and surface-mount components. The profile has short dwell time in the solder pot and high preheat to minimize thermal shock in ceramic components and temperature within resin molded parts.

B. Reflow soldering has the highest yields due to controlled heating rates and solder liquidus times. Only the dwell time and peak temperature limitations of resin molded components need to be considered.

C. Hand soldering techniques require the use of a heat sink on leads to minimize the heat damage to the component.

Application Information

In general, semiconductor diodes are used as:
- Rectifiers
- Switchers
- Varactors
- Voltage stabilizers.

The term diode and rectifier can be used interchangeably. A diode usually refers to a small signal device with current typically in the milli-amp range. A rectifier is a power device conducting from 1 to 1000 amps or more.

The minimal diode specifications required are:
- Package style
- Rated forward current
- Maximum reverse voltage
- Maximum leakage current
- Maximum forward voltage drop
- Maximum reverse recovery time.

Diode schematic symbol and polarity marking.

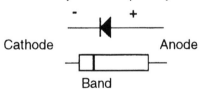

Germanium Diodes

Basically, early semiconductor developments used germanium as the commercial semiconductor material. Later, silicon became the semiconductor of choice due to its more stable temperature characteristics and ease of processing. As a consequence of that, most early germanium diode and transistor semiconductors were replaced with silicon.

Germanium diodes have the advantage of an intrinsically low forward voltage drop, typically 0.3 volts; this low forward voltage drop results in a low power loss and a more efficient diode; making it superior in many ways to the silicon diode. By comparison, a silicon diode forward voltage drop is typically 0.7 volts.

This lower voltage drop with germanium becomes important in:
- Low level logic circuits
- Very low signal environments (signal detection from audio to FM frequencies).

As a result, germanium diodes are finding increasing application in low level digital circuits. In these low voltage applications, a Schottky diode could also be used.

With this increased interest, certain general germanium characteristics should be understood. First and most important is that of an increased leakage current for germanium at a reverse voltage. This is mitigated to some degree by the fact that in low level circuits, the reverse voltage applied to a germanium diode is also usually very low, resulting in a low reverse leakage current (leakage current is directly proportional to reverse voltage). However, the leakage current is still larger than with silicon. A properly designed circuit can lessen this factor.

Silicon Diodes

Small Signal Diodes are utilized for:
- Routing
- Switching
- Signal blocking.

Product usage includes:
- Power supplies
- Automotive systems
- Printed circuit motherboards
- Telecommunications equipment.

Silicon is a particularly suitable material for the manufacture of diodes because of the small leakage currents, high breakdown voltages, and steep forward characteristics that may be attained. Admissible junction temperatures of up to $T_j = +200°C$ allow a relatively high level of power to be dissipated in a package of small dimensions. Silicon diodes are manufactured as junction diodes by a diffusion process, preferably using the epitaxial planar technique.

Since a certain amount of the generated heat must be conducted away from the junction via the connecting leads, the following proviso is often quoted in data sheets: "Valid provided that leads are kept at ambient temperature at a distance of 4 mm from case."

A 3-leaded diode package may have one of the following configurations:
- Single diode.
- Dual common anode.
- Dual anode to cathode.
- Dual diode with common cathode.

Silicon Capacitance Diodes

Silicon capacitance diodes (also called Varactors) are used for:
- Mixing
- Frequency modulation
- Frequency multiplication
- Electronic tuning purposes
- Dielectric and parametric amplifiers
- Automatic Frequency Control (AFC)
- Controlling the bandwidth of capacitively coupled bandpass filters.

In all these applications, advantage is taken of the fact that the depletion layer capacitance is dependent on the applied reverse voltage.

Basically, a silicon capacitance diode has the same construction as any normal alloyed or diffused semiconductor diode. The depletion layer of the PN junction contains only very few free charge carriers and can be considered as the dielectric of a capacitor whose plates are formed by the high-conductivity regions. Silicon capacitance diodes are normally operated under reverse bias conditions. If the applied reverse voltage is increased, then the thickness of the depletion layer increases and the depletion layer capacitance consequently decreases.

These so-called "large capacitance ratio" or tuner (varactor) diodes have a hyperabrupt (retrograded) PN junction giving a steep capacitance characteristic. This makes it possible for the first time to cover the entire frequency range of a VHF or UHF television tuner, or that of a MW receiver, without any band switching. The capacitance variation of these tuner diodes does not follow a mathematically definable law. To ensure accurate tracking, therefore, diodes intended for incorporation into tuners are supplied in matched groups.

Another important parameter of a capacitance diode is the Q factor, which should be high. At high frequencies, the Q factor of a capacitance diode is:

$$Q = \frac{1}{2 \pi f C_{tot} r_s}$$

where:
C_{tot} = diode capacitance.
r_s = series resistance of the diode. The series resistance r_s, is virtually the same as the bulk resistance of the diode.

As can be deduced from the Q formula, the Q factor of a capacitance diode varies with reverse bias; this is because the diode capacitance decreases as the reverse voltage is increased; the Q factor is also dependent on frequency.

The "cut-off" frequency, f_{Q1}, of a capacitance diode is that frequency at which the Q factor is reduced to 1, that is:

$$Q = \frac{f_{Q1}}{f}$$

Another important factor which cannot be altogether ignored is the series inductance, L_s. This comprises the inductance of the connecting leads and the internal inductance of the diode. The inductance, L_s, together with the diode capacitance, C_{tot}, forms a series-tuned circuit which resonates at a frequency of:

$$f_o = \frac{1}{2 \pi \sqrt{L_s \times C_{tot}}}$$

Depending on the application, a capacitance diode can be represented by an equivalent circuit which consists of:
- The diode capacitance C_{tot}, a series resistance r_s, a series inductance L_s, and a reverse resistance $R = V_R/I_R$.
- Since the reverse resistance of a silicon diode is extremely high, it is usually ignored, and the circuit then omits R.

At low (30kHz to 300kHz) and medium (300kHz to 3MHz) frequencies the series inductance, L_s, can also be ignored.

Junction capacitance, series resistance, and reverse resistance are temperature dependent. The temperature coefficient of the junction capacitance is due to the effect of the temperature on the diffusion voltage which is -2mV/°C. This means that a reverse voltage reduction of approximately 2mV has the same effect on the junction capacitance as a junction ternperature increase of 1°C. The temperature coefficient of the junction capacitance is therefore positive, and decreases as the reverse bias is increased. The reverse resistance decreases by about 6% and the series resistance decreases by about 1% if the junction temperature is increased by 1°C.

To ensure that the reverse bias does not vary appreciably with temperature, it is good practice to make the value of the diode series resistor through which the reverse bias is applied as low as practicable (approx. 30 to 100kΩ).

In all tuning applications it is important that the AC signal amplitude is small in comparison with the lowest reverse bias voltage applied, as otherwise, the nonlinearity of the capacitance characteristic will cause signal distortion and an apparent change of capacitance. By the use of two diodes in a push-pull arrangement it is possible to obtain a considerable reduction in distortion, even at large signal amplitudes because the diodes are then driven in antiphase and thus tend to cancel any distortion.

Current Regulator Diodes

Current regulator diodes are designed to maximize diode output impedance and temperature stability for the most demanding applications. These diodes are used where the circuit requires simple "floating" operation with no biasing voltages or additional components. These diodes are ideal in simple timing circuits.

Applications are where low-voltage current sources and/or current limiting are needed in portable test equipment and other instrumentation.

Low-Leakage Pico-Amp Diodes

These diodes offer circuit input protection in the most critical applications by combining extremely low pico-amp leakage with low capacitance.

Key applications include high-performance instrumentation and noisy electrical environments. The diodes clamp unwanted voltage spikes in high-gain circuits that would otherwise lead to false data and/or saturation of an op-amp. These diodes also provide multiplexer overload protection. The diodes are transparent to the circuit, except when protection is needed.

Packaging may contain either a single or a dual diode configuration.

Silicon Diode Switches

These diodes were developed for:
- Electronic band switching in television and radio tuners operating at UHF to microwave.

Diode switches, unlike the switching diodes normally used for logic applications (for example: 1N4148 or similar), are intended as an electronic equivalent to the contacts of mechanical range switches.

Diode switches exhibit either a very high reverse impedance (approx. $1M\Omega$ in parallel with approx. 1.3pF) when they are nonconducting (switch open), or a very low dynamic forward impedance (approx. 0.5Ω in series with approx. 2.5nH) when they are conducting (switch closed).

The construction of the diode switches ensures that full advantage can be taken of their inherently small series inductance, since connecting leads or electrodes may be soldered directly to the case.

Surface-Mount Chip Diodes

Chips are leadless silicon die with glass passivation. They are hermetic, noncavity parts. Top and bottom terminations are gold or aluminum plated. The die can be supplied with or without straps for the top connection and can be mounted using solder paste or conductive epoxy. When using the strapped die, the land pattern shown in the data sheets can be used to design PC boards or substrate plating. The straps are bonded to the chip utilizing very high temperature solder. The melting point of this is slightly higher than 300°C. When placing these parts on a PC board or substrate care should be taken not to exceed 260°C. If possible, it is recommended that design calculations not exceed a junction temperature of 150°C. While the chip itself can readily withstand temperatures up to 600°C, the solders available cannot. When using the nonstrapped version of the die, an alternate method of making the top connection, such as wire bonding, must be used.

Diode Arrays

Multiple diode packaging or diode arrays have been an important semiconductor product. The diode array saves assembly time and improve reliability over individually packaged diodes. The term diode array implies that four or more diodes are in a single package. The most efficient packaging scheme is typically eight diodes or more in a dual-inline-package (DIP).

Other packages are the single-inline-package (SIP), the flat pack, and even a surface-mount diode array. Although multiple diode arrays incorporate different type diodes, the most popular arrays incorporate a fast, small signal diode such as the 1N4148. The core driver arrays employ a fast switching, higher current diode. If two independent leads are brought out for each diode, a sixteen leaded DIP would be fully utilized. On the other hand, if a common cathode or common anode connection was used, internally a sixteen pin DIP would accommodate fourteen diodes. Other common connections are available.

Glass Passivated Rectifiers

The glass passivated rectifier is a hermetically sealed, cavity free, diffused junction rectifier with unsurpassed operating and surge capabilities at high temperatures. An extremely pure specially developed glass applied in direct contact with the silicon junction creates an ideal cavity-free passivating medium.

The materials (glass-silicon-molybdenum) in the device were carefully developed to be thermally matched to ensure uniform expansion characteristics over a broad range of temperature extremes. Furthermore, only high temperature brazing operations and a glass fusing process performed in excess of 600°C are utilized in the construction of this device. These techniques eliminate solder construction and tremendously enhances mechanical strength and temperature cycling capability. This results in increased operating and storage temperature ranges while reducing thermal resistance.

Hermetically sealed glass passivated junction diodes are normally available in an axial leaded package only.

Glass Passivated Die Level Rectifiers

This type of rectifier utilizes glass passivation on the chip level to enhance its device's performance. The difference is that the glass is applied to the wafer prior to die cutting to achieve optimum protection of the part without an individual glass slurry application. This system achieves excellent reliability capabilities while lending itself to high volume manufacturing. This technology is available in both axial and surface-mount packages.

DIACs

The diac is a bidirectional trigger diode which is designed specifically to trigger a triac or SCR. The diac is a bidirectional thryistor. The diac does not conduct (except for a small leakage current) until the breakover voltage is reached. Once it is triggered from blocking to conduction, the diac goes into avalanche conduction while the device exhibits a negative resistance characteristic and the voltage drop across the diac snaps back, creating a breakover current sufficient to trigger a triac or SCR. The diac demonstrates low breakover current at breakover voltage and withstands peak pulse current. Although most diacs have symmetric switching voltages, asymmetric diacs are available.

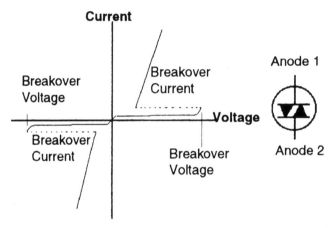

Typical Diac characteristic curve and schematic symbol.

Diacs main characteristics are:
- Breakover voltage
- Voltage symmetry
- Breakback voltage
- Breakover current
- Power dissipation.

Diacs are intended for use in thyristor phase control circuits for:
- Heat controls
- Lamp dimming
- Universal motor speed controls.

PIN Diodes

PIN stands for P-Intrinsic-N. This type of diode has a highly doped "P" region and a highly doped "N" region separated by a lightly doped layer of high resistivity material which is nearly intrinsic "I" or pure.

The PIN diode, under reverse bias, has a very high impedance (at microwave frequencies) whereas at moderate forward current it has a very low impedance. This permits the use of the PIN diode as a low-loss switch with small self-capacitance. The PIN diode can also be used as a high-frequency attenuator in a pi- or T-circuit because the RF resistance of the diode can be varied from large to small values by changing the diode bias.

PIN diodes are used primarily for the control of RF and microwave signals. Applications include:
- Limiting
- Switching
- Attenuating
- Modulating
- Phase shifting.

Schottky Rectifiers

Low forward voltage drop and fast switching make these diodes ideal for:
- Motor controllers.
- Click suppression.
- Polarity protection applications.
- Protection of MOS integrated circuits.
- Low-voltage, high frequency inverters.
- Efficient full-wave bridges in telephone subsets.
- Portable electronics power management circuits.
- High current rectification in switch-mode power supplies.
- Blocking diodes in rechargeable low-voltage battery systems.
- Steering, biasing, and coupling for fast switching and low logic level applications.

Dual Schottky diodes in one package, when connected in the common-cathode configuration, provide the complete output rectifier function of the common transformer "center tap" and "forward" rectifier circuits in a single package.

Low capacitance Schottky diodes can be used in:
- TVs
- Radios
- Detectors and fast switching up to 1GHz
- Hyper-band tuners when used in phase detectors, single, double, and ring balanced mixers in narrowband receivers up to 1GHz.

Silicon Schottky diode current flow is due to majority carrier conduction. It is not affected by reverse recovery transients as are conventional PN diodes due to stored charge and minority carrier injection.

Schottky rectifiers have been used in the power supply industry for decades. The primary assets of Schottky devices are switching speeds approaching zero-time and very low forward voltage drop. This combination makes Schottky barrier rectifiers ideal for the output stages of switching power supplies. On the negative side, Schottky devices are also known for limited high-temperature operation, high leakage, and limited voltage range. Though these limitations exist, they are quantifiable and controllable, allowing wide application of these devices in switch-mode power supplies.

A Schottky rectifier is the ideal product for high speed and low power loss applications. Their metal-silicon junctions and majority carrier condition results in extremely fast recovery times and very low forward voltage drops. A sputtered metalization process and ion implanted guardring technology results in a highly reliable Schottky product. The sputtering technique provides a very uniform Schottky junction, yielding a well controlled barrier height distribution. Ion implantation provides consistency to the PN junction guardring, resulting in reverse energy handling capability. These devices are protected by an PN junction guardring and against excessive voltage, such as electro-static discharges. Schottky barrier rectifier's high-temperature leakage and forward voltage drop are controlled by two primary factors: the size of the chip's active area and the barrier height.

Lower barrier heights result in lower forward drop and improved power dissipation. This is at the expense of high temperature leakage current due to the physics of the Schottky barrier junction. Conversely, high barrier heights result in improved high temperature leakage at the expense of higher forward voltage drop. These parameters are also controlled by the die size and resistivity of the starting material. A larger die will lower the forward voltage but raise the leakage if all other parameters are held constant. The resistivity of the starting material must be chosen in a range where the breakdown voltage is not degraded at the low end and the forward end of the resistivity range. Since a larger chip size is obviously more expensive, this is not the primary method for controlling these parameters. Chip size is usually set to a dimension where the current density through the die is kept at a safe level.

Silicon Controlled Rectifiers (SCR)

The Silicon Controlled Rectifier (SCR) is a thyristor. A thyristor is a conventional rectifier controlled by a gate signal. The main circuit is a rectifier. When the application of a forward voltage is not enough for conduction, an applied gate signal controls the rectifier conduction.

SCR applications include the following circuits:
- Inverter
- Chopper
- Phase control
- Power switching.

Major parameters for specifying a SCR are:
- Maximum dV/dt
- Power dissipation
- Peak forward voltage
- Minimum holding current
- Maximum forward current
- Reverse breakdown voltage
- Gate trigger voltage and current.

V-I characteristic curve of a SCR with gate open and symbol.

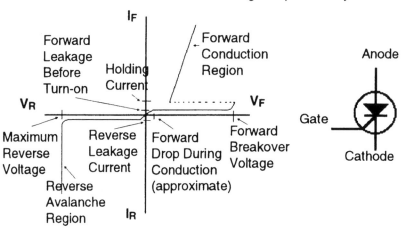

In the forward direction with open gate, the SCR remains in an OFF condition (there is a small forward leakage) up until the forward breakover voltage is reached. At that point, the curve snaps back to a typical forward diode characteristic. The application of a small forward gate voltage switches the SCR onto its standard diode forward characteristic for voltages less that the forward breakover voltage. The reverse characteristics are the same as for a typical diode or rectifier; a breakover voltage with its avalanche current and a leakage current for voltages less than the breakover voltage.

The rectifier circuit (anode-cathode) has a low forward resistance and a high reverse resistance. It is controlled from an OFF state (high resistance) to the ON state (low resistance) by a signal applied to a third terminal called the gate. Once it is turned ON, it remains ON even after removal of the gate signal, as long as a minimum current, the hold current, (Ih), is maintained in the main or rectifier circuit. To turn OFF the SCR, the anode-cathode current must be reduced to less than the holding current, Ih.

The SCR can also be switched by exceeding the forward breakover voltage, but this is usually considered a design limitation and switching is normally controlled with a gate voltage. One serious limitation of the SCR is the rate of rise of voltage with respect to time (dV/dt). A large rate of rise of circuit voltage can trigger an SCR into conduction. This is a circuit design concern.

Transient Voltage Suppressors (TVS)

Transient Voltage Suppressors (TVS) are semiconductor devices designed to provide protection against voltage and current transients. The silicon TVS is designed to operate in the avalanche mode and uses a large junction area to absorb large transient currents. Operation in the avalanche mode insures a low impedance. The TVS is also characterized by a fast response time. The TVS is available as unipolar or bipolar; that is, the TVS can suppress transients in one direction or in both directions.

Typical characteristic curve for a bipolar TVS and symbols.

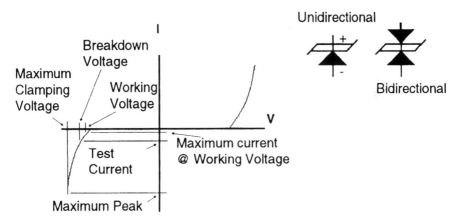

The breakdown voltage is the point the TVS device enters avalanche, a high conductance region. This voltage is measured at a test current. A circuit with a TVS protection would operate below the working voltage. The maximum clamping voltage is the maximum voltage across the TVS when it is subjected to the maximum peak current

Transient voltage suppressors are specialized zener diodes intended to clamp the voltage appearing across a line, thereby preventing transient spikes from damaging sensitive components. The device accomplish this by conducting when the voltage across the line exceeds the zener-avalanche rating. This physical design enables these avalanche diodes to absorb large amounts of energy for short time durations without sustaining damage.

Because transient voltages can be quite high, suppressors must be able to handle large avalanche currents. This means that care must be taken in the construction of the package and assembly process to ensure that the suppressor can tolerate high energy levels for short periods.

When used within each component's power handling capability, transient voltage suppressors do not exhibit a wear out mechanism as many metal-oxide-varistors (MOVs) and similar technologies do. The TVS also has sub-nanosecond turn-on times and superior clamping characteristics when compared to MOVs.

Transient voltage suppressors have excellent clamping capability that can protect devices against transient voltages generated by lightning, Electro-Static Discharge (ESD), inductive load switching, and Nuclear Electro-Magnetic Pulse (NEMP) from a nuclear explosion. Often, a 1500 watt peak pulse rated device will protect against transients due to secondary lightning effects or inductive switching on power, data, and telephone lines. A 500 watt device is sufficient to protect sensitive components against transients generated by electro-static discharge.

The suppressor should be as physically close to the vulnerable component's ground return as possible. The lower the parasitic inductance between the ground plane of the component to be protected and the TVS, the more effective the suppressor will be. Under high current pulse conditions, excessive lead lengths on suppressor components can be responsible for destruction of the protected circuit. This is caused by voltage build-up across the small but finite amount of inductance in the interconnecting leads of the protector.

TVS diodes protect:
- Telecom circuits
- Computer power supplies
- Aircraft avionics and controls
- Computer data and buss line circuits.

A TVS in the signal and input power lines prevents microprocessor system failures caused by transients (electro-static charges), AC power surges, power supply reversals, or during switching of the power supply to ON or OFF. Placing TVSs across the signal lines to ground will keep unwanted transients out of the data buss and control buss. The TVS, when shunted across the power lines, maintains a continuous operating voltage during AC line surges and switching transients.

High immunity and super-high immunity circuits are prone to damage by noise transients as a result of the power being dissipated by the substrate input diode. Excess current passing through the input diode can cause an open circuit condition or slow degradation of circuit performance. A TVS located on the signal line can absorb this excess energy. For some circuit applications, a low-capacitance device may be required.

The TVS can protect the internal MOSFET from transients introduced on the power supply line. A common practice is to place a series protection diode from source to gate, but this does not offer protection from source to ground and is usually limited on peak power dissipation. A TVS is required on each voltage supply line to the integrated circuit.

Totem pole output circuits often generate current spikes requiring decoupling capacitors. While maintaining circuit continuity, the TVS is capable of absorbing the energy pulse as well as eliminating noise spikes due to such things as cross-talk, etc. A clamp diode in the IC substrate is limited in conduction current providing minimum protection.

The TVS placed in the output of a voltage regulator can often replace many components associated with a protection circuit such as a crowbar circuit. It may also be required to protect the bypass transistor from voltage spikes across the collector to emitter terminals.

A TVS on the output of an op-amp will prevent a voltage transient, due to a short circuit or an inductive load, from being transmitted into the output stage.

Very high transient voltages are generated when an inductive load is disconnected, such as motors, relay coils, and solenoids. The TVS provides protection for the output transistor as well as the IC, eliminating a resistor/capacitor network.

Transient voltage suppressors can be used in series or parallel to increase their power handling capability. No precautions are required when using transient voltage suppressors in a series string since power dissipation for two or more devices of the same type is equally shared. When using transient voltage suppressors in parallel, it is necessary for the devices to be closely matched (approx. 0.1V of each other) in order for equal sharing to take place. Matched sets can be requested from device manufacturers.

Transient voltage suppressors can be a unidirectional or bidirectional type. A bidirectional type is ideal for LAN protection applications.

Automotive transient voltage suppressors are designed for stability and power handling capability over the entire automotive temperature range and beyond. Under-the-hood applications include alternator rectifiers, protection of automotive electrical systems from automotive "load dump" transients, and other unexpected surges within the electrical system.

Tuner/Bandswitching Diodes

Tuner diodes are variable capacitance diodes (varactors) used for the tuning of VHF, UHF, cable, and direct satellite television bands. Electronic bandswitching diodes are used in radio and television tuners within the frequency range of 50MHz to 1GHz. Tuner diodes are typically used for direct satellite receivers.

Tuner diodes are available as singles or as matched sets of two or more units according to the tracking condition required.

Triacs

The triac is a three-terminal thyristor device for controlling current in either direction. A triac operates in the same way as a SCR , but it operates in both a forward and reverse direction. The triac symbol is two SCRs in parallel connected in the opposite direction, with only one trigger or gate terminal. The main or power terminals are designated as MT1 and MT2. When the voltage on MT2 is positive with regard to MT1 and a positive gate voltage is applied, the *left* SCR conducts. When the voltage is reversed and a negative voltage is applied to the gate, the *right* SCR conducts. Minimum holding current (Ih), must be maintained in order to keep a triac conducting.

Typical triac V-I characteristic curve and symbol.

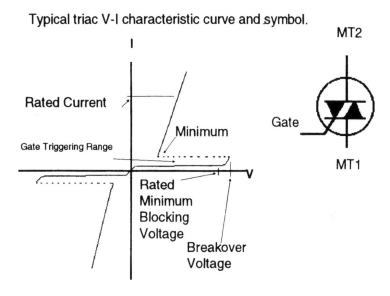

A triac can be triggered into conduction by either a plus (+) or minus (-) gate signal. A triac can also be triggered by exceeding the breakover voltage. This is not normally done in triac circuit operation because the breakover voltage is usually considered a limitation during design. The other major limitation, as with the SCR, is the rate of rise of voltage with respect to time (dV/dt). A triac can be switched into conduction by a large dV/dt.

Triac major specifications are:
- Gate voltage
- Forward voltage
- Switching speed
- Maximum dV/dt
- Maximum current
- Minimum holding current
- Reverse breakover voltage
- Gate current trigger requirements.

Typical triac applications:
- Phase control
- AC switching
- Inverter design
- Relay replacement.

Tunnel Diodes

A tunnel diode is a semiconductor with a negative resistance region that results in very fast switching speeds, up to 5GHz. The operation depends upon a quantum principle known as "tunneling." The intrinsic voltage barrier (0.3V for germanium junctions) is reduced due to doping levels which enhance tunneling.

Highly doped material of an PN junction diode develops a condition where the electrons tunnel through the junction with the speed of light, rather than overcome the barrier effect. This allows operation at super-high frequencies. The tunnel diode has a sharp reverse-bias current curve. The reverse breakdown voltage for tunnel diodes is very low, typically 200mV. The tunnel diode conducts very heavily at the reverse breakdown voltage.

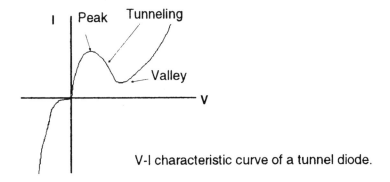

V-I characteristic curve of a tunnel diode.

The negative resistance region is the major characteristic for the tunnel diode. In this region, as the voltage is increased, the current decreases; just the opposite of a conventional diode.

Tunnel diode major specifications are:
- Peak voltage
- Peak current
- Valley voltage
- Valley current.

The tunnel diode can operate as an:
- Amplifier
- Oscillator, or
- Reverse-direction, low-voltage rectifier.

Back Diodes

Back diodes are a tunnel diode with a suppressed peak current characteristic. The back diode conducts to a lesser degree than the tunnel diode in the forward direction. It is the operation between the start and full conduction that makes the back diode useful. Forward conduction typically begins at 300mV (for germanium) and a voltage increase of only 500mV may be required for full range operation.

V-I characteristic curve for a back diode.

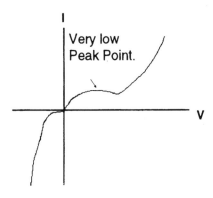

Varactor Diodes

Varactor diodes are also silicon capacitance diodes. In all these applications, the basic variation of junction capacitance with reverse voltage has been taken into consideration. When a reverse voltage is applied to a PN junction, the holes in the P-region are attached to the cathode terminal creating a region where there is little current. This region, (the depletion region), is essentially devoid of carriers and behaves like the dielectric of a capacitor.

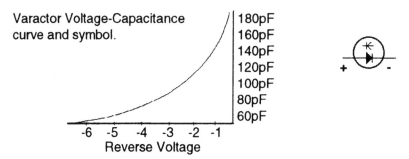

Varactor Voltage-Capacitance curve and symbol.

The depletion region increases as reverse voltage across it increases; and since capacitance varies inversely as dielectric thickness, the junction capacitance will decrease as the voltage across the PN junction increases. So by varying the reverse voltage across the PN junction, the junction capacitance can be varied. Refer to silicon capacitance diodes section.

Varactor diode considerations are
- Voltage
- Leakage current
- Capacitance value
- Maximum working voltage
- Variation in capacitance with voltage.

Varactor diodes are used in circuits such as:
- Tuning
- Modulation
- Frequency multiplier
- Parametric amplification
- Automatic Frequency Control (AFC)
- Switching in the VHF and microwave regions
- Couple element in filters with controlled bandwidth.

Zener Diodes

A zener diode is used in the reverse characteristic quadrant of the diode curve. As the reverse voltage is increased, the leakage current remains essentially constant until the breakdown voltage is reached. The breakdown voltage is where the current increases dramatically. This breakdown voltage is the zener voltage for zener diodes. For the conventional diode it is imperative to operate below this voltage, however, the zener diode is intended to operate at the breakdown voltage. Because of this, zener diodes are excellent choices for voltage regulator applications.

Silicon zener diode V-I characteristic curve and symbol.

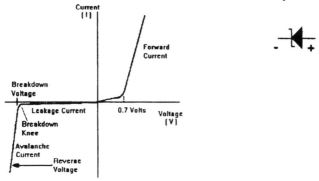

Zener diode basic parameters that must be specified are:
- Zener voltage
- Zener resistance
- Power handling capability
- Tolerance of the specified voltage

Note: A test current must be specified with the voltage and tolerance.

Zener diodes utilize controlled avalanche technology (silicon epitaxial planar construction) to provide stable voltage references throughout a specified current range for electronic circuits. Zener diodes are available in various power ratings, different package styles, and with voltage tolerances as tight as +/-5%. A zener diode meets most voltage reference needs.

Zener diode applications include:
- Voltage limiting
- Voltage regulation
- Voltage surge absorption.

Basic Circuits

Diodes used as an OR gate.

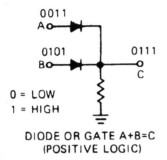

DIODE OR GATE A+B=C
(POSITIVE LOGIC)

Zener diode for voltage regulation.

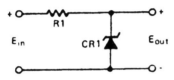

Chapter 2

High-Voltage Rectifiers

The ideal high-voltage rectifier is a single-junction diode that blocks the required voltage quickly without leaking reverse current and generates no heat from forward power losses. However, in real world rectifiers there are complex trade-offs. The basic choice is between strings of single-junction silicon diodes or a multi-junction high-voltage silicon diode.

There are different approaches to creating high-voltage rectifiers. One approach involves connecting a number of lower-voltage single-junction diodes in series. The simplest, called a high-voltage stick, consists of the required number of diodes tied end to end. However, when creating a series string, it is important to consider such factors as voltage sharing, junction temperature, and matching reverse-recovery characteristics. To account for these factors, compensation networks consisting of resistor/capacitor strings are frequently employed. The resulting network, called an R/C-compensated diode string, is usually used in applications where the power exceeds 30 watts. At lower power levels, such as those encountered in CRT power supplies, multi-junction diodes are used.

Another approach is the deep-diffused junction. This approach is ideal for high-voltage, multi-junction designs. The greatest advantage of the multi-junction process is the capability of stacking diodes at the wafer stage, thus allowing high-temperature bonding and reducing metallization between wafers to almost zero. Moreover, fabricating all the diode junctions on the same wafer provides a simple method of matching junction characteristics.

Forward drop in high-voltage rectifiers is usually not as important an issue as it is in low-voltage applications. Consider, for example, a 1000-watt, 5-volt power supply. If its rectifiers exhibit a 0.7 volt forward drop, the power loss with 200 amps flowing would be 140 watts, or 14 percent of the power being handled. In contrast, the rectifier's forward drop in a typical 1000 watt-1000 volt supply ranges between 1.0 and 1.5 volts. At full output, the current is 1.0 amp, which with a 1.5 volt forward drop, translates to a 1.5 watt power loss. This represents less than two-tenths of one percent of the power being passed through the rectifier.

In applications, reverse recovery time (t_{rr}) factors translate into high-voltage junctions having slower recovery times than similarly doped low-voltage junctions. Because of this, high-voltage junctions typically contain considerably higher concentrations of dopants like platinum or gold than do similar-speed low-voltage junctions. These higher dopant concentrations result in higher forward voltage drops and reverse leakage currents.

All of the items discussed may be considered and yet problems may still occur due to a lack of understanding of the application. Outside factors can influence failure and even mask the failure mode.

REVERSE LEAKAGE
Power diodes with high-voltage junctions differ from their low-voltage counterparts. At room temperature, the dominant leakage path is usually along the surface while current, due to junction capacitance, is much lower in amplitude. Careful attention to the leakage source is important. It is quite common, for example, to carefully match the reverse current measurements of diodes that are then connected in a string at 25°C. When the diodes are subjected to elevated temperatures, it is probable that the reverse current flowing through the diodes at even slightly elevated temperatures would change significantly and produce a severe mismatch. This, in turn, would result in an over-voltage condition on some diodes.

To illustrate how this can happen, consider a situation in which two diodes exhibit exactly the same reverse current at 25°C.

Example:

	$T_{amb} = +25°C$	$T_{amb} = +100°C$
Diode 1	$I_R(\text{diffusion}) = 10\ nA$ $+ I_R(\text{surface}) = 500nA$ $I_R(\text{total}) = 510nA$	$I_R(\text{diffusion}) = 15\mu A$ $+ I_R(\text{surface}) = 500nA$ $I_R(\text{total}) = 15.5\mu A$
Diode 2	$I_R(\text{diffusion}) = 500nA$ $+ I_R(\text{surface}) = 10nA$ $I_R(\text{total}) = 510nA$	$I_R(\text{diffusion}) = 75\mu A$ $+ I_R(\text{surface}) = 10nA$ $I_R(\text{total}) = 75.1\mu A$

As shown above, a pair of diodes that were perfectly matched at 25°C would be terribly mismatched at higher temperatures.

MULTI-JUNCTION REVERSE RECOVERY TIME

Deep-diffused multi-junction diodes ideally address the problem of individual diodes with mismatched reverse recovery times. The question is, how does one prevent the fastest diode from seeing all of the reverse voltage while the other diodes are recovering? As stated earlier, reverse recovery time varies with temperature, resistivity, and dopant concentrations. The concentric use of matched wafers ensures closely matched dice that track with temperature much better than discrete diodes. Also, each die can survive while operating in the reverse avalanche mode in the event that one chip recovers slightly faster than another.

The worst-case temperature of the center junction is often perceived as an uncontrollable, frightening condition when it is, in fact, merely a matter of thermal management. Silicon is a very good conductor that compares favorably with some aluminum alloys. As a result, it provides an efficient thermal path through the multi-junction stack to the leads.

An important factor in any high-voltage application is corona; a partial discharge that results from ionization of air in a gap that is under voltage stress. Over time, the presence of corona destroys insulation and is particularly destructive in trapped-air voids near high-voltage sources. The geometry of the multi-junction deep-diffused diode is cylindrical and void-free. Moreover, it is not subjected to corona if it is encapsulated in a dielectric. Also, the replacement of several diodes with a single multi-junction diode often leads to substantially fewer corona problems in potted assemblies because unnecessary air traps are eliminated.

High-voltage rectification presents unique challenges to the designer. Careful examination of the application requirements must be made to choose the proper solution for size, cost, and reliability. Diode parameters are interdependent and require a completely different thought process when considering high-voltage diodes than when choosing their low-voltage counterparts. Stray parameters become major influences with high-voltage. Diodes become more temperature dependent and mismatches become more significant. Because of these factors, deep-diffused multi-junction diodes offer solutions to many high-voltage rectification problems.

Thermal Analysis

Controlling junction temperature is key to reliable design in any semiconductor package. Heat is primarily generated by losses in the silicon junction(s) of the rectifying diodes. It is often difficult to anticipate the magnitude of heat loss as the heat source varies considerably with the application. High-voltage diodes present unique problems that must be addressed.

In high-voltage diodes, internal heat is generated primarily by:
- Forward voltage
- Reverse leakage current
- Reverse recovery losses.

Each of these factors change differently with temperature and must be considered carefully over the intended operating temperature range.

TOTAL heat source consideration must be made. The deceptive difference in recovery losses in high-voltage applications is due primarily to the high-voltage bias applied while the diode is recovering from forward bias to a blocking mode.

This can be minimized by:
- Improving the thermal impedance
- Decreasing the forward voltage losses,
- Decreasing the reverse recovery losses, or
- Operating over a reduced temperature range.

Forward voltage and reverse recovery losses are dependent on the diode used in the circuit and on the circuit characteristics. In many cases, there are trade-offs to any changes made in diode characteristics. For instance, decreasing reverse recovery time in a diode will generally increase its forward voltage. Or, reducing the reverse blocking voltage of a diode to reduce forward voltage may increase the risk of exceeding the voltage rating of the part.

Once the diode has been selected for an application, the thermal impedance of the diode package must be optimized. Thermal impedance in a rectifier is the resistance to the movement of heat energy from the junction of the rectifier to a heat sink or reservoir used to dissipate the heat. The thermal path for the rectifier will vary depending on the packaging configuration of the part. Typical schemes will now be discussed in detail.

Diode Mounted on a PC Board

The two major thermal paths for a diode mounted to a printed circuit (PC) board are through the diode leads to the PC board and through the diode body and leads to the surrounding air or other medium.

The thermal resistances of diodes are given for several lead lengths in the diode data sheets. Multiplying the thermal resistance of a diode through its leads by the power dissipated in the diode will give its junction temperature rise over the temperature of its mounting location. The temperature or thermal impedance of the diode mounting location will have a major effect on the junction temperature of the diode since any temperature rise of the mounting location will be added to the temperature rise of the diode itself.

The medium surrounding the diode can reduce the junction temperature of the diode by adding a parallel thermal path. If the surrounding medium is air, its cooling effect will depend largely on its temperature and on its movement. Whereas forced air can significantly reduce the junction temperature of a diode, the cooling effect of still air, such as would be the case if the diode is mounted in an enclosed box, may have little effect on the junction temperature of the diode. If the surrounding medium is a potting material, its cooling effect will depend on the temperature and thermal conductivity of the material, the power dissipation of any components located near the diode, and on the thermal path through the material to any outside surface or heat sink.

Surface-Mounted Diode
In a surface-mount diode application, the diode is mounted to a ceramic substrate or PC board. The heat generated in the junction of the diode flows through the end tabs directly to the substrate or PC board. The thermal impedance of the diode (given in the diode data sheet) is added to the thermal resistance of the substrate or PC board to obtain the total thermal impedance of the package.

Diode Operating in Oil
For a diode operating in oil, the heat generated in the diode will mostly be dissipated to the oil through the leads of the diode. A small percentage of the heat will also be dissipated to the oil through the body of the diode. The zero lead length thermal impedance as specified by the data sheet for the diode can be used as a maximum thermal impedance from the diode to the oil. The diode junction temperature rise over the oil temperature will be equal to the power dissipated in the diode times the thermal resistance of the diode to the oil. Typically, oil operation provides a very good method of removing the heat from the diode.

Diode Encapsulated in a Potting Material
With a diode encapsulated in a potting material, the heat generated in the diode must be dissipated through the material to an outside surface or heat sink. The thermal conductivity of the potting material used can be very critical. The thermal conductivities of silicon potting materials are typically lower than those of rigid epoxies, although there are some factors that may make the use of a silicon potting material more desirable. Other material, such as glass or alumina, can be added to the potting material to increase its thermal conductivity. Thermal conductivities for various materials are given in Table 1.

TABLE 1 - Materials Commonly Used in Potted Rectifier Assemblies.

Material	Thermal Conductivity W/IN°C	Linear Thermal Expansion ppm/°C
Silver 99.9%	10.500	23.5
Copper OFC	10.000	17.0
Tungsten	4.250	4.5
Aluminum 6061T6	3.96	23.5
Silicon (pure)	3.700	3.0
Molybdenum	3.400	5.1
Beryllia 95%	3.000	7.5
Tin	1.600	23.5
Solder 63Sn-37Pb	1.270	25.0
Alumina 96%	0.890	6.4
Lead	0.880	29.0
Solder 96.5Sn-3.5Ag	0.840	30.0
Epoxy Stycast 2850KT	0.106	28.8
Epoxy Stycast 2850MT	0.075	29.2
PC Board G-10 (unclad)	0.052	21.1
Epoxy Stycast 2850FT	0.036	29.0
RTV 1200HTC	0.036	80.0
Glass	0.031	3.3
Epoxy Scotchcast 281	0.013	150.0
RTV 3120	0.008	350.0
RTV 615	0.005	270.0

Thermal Impedance Formula (for conduction):

$$Q = \frac{\sigma \times A \times T}{L} \quad \text{or} \quad \Theta = \frac{L}{\sigma \times A}$$

where:

Q = Heat conducted (watts).

A = Cross sectional area of heat path (in^2).

σ = Thermal conductivity (watts/in^2 x°C).

L = Length of heat path (in).

T = Temperature difference, $T_1 - T_2$.

Θ = Thermal resistance (°C/watt).

Along with the thermal conductivity of the potting material used, the mechanical configuration or layout of the diode in the package will have an effect on thermal impedance. The formula used for thermal impedance is:

$$\Theta jc = \frac{L}{\sigma \times A}$$

where:
- Θjc = thermal impedance from diode to heat sink or outside surface.
- A = area of the thermal path.
- σ = thermal conductivity of the material as given in Table 1.
- L = length of the thermal path from the diode to the to the heat sink.

In many practical cases, the area or length of a thermal path may be difficult to determine exactly. Also, in some cases there are several thermal paths that must be considered in parallel. The above formula should be used to arrive at a close approximation of the thermal impedance of the package, followed by an actual test of the junction temperature of the diodes in the package.

As the above formula indicates, thermal impedance is inversely proportional to the thermal area, so that thermal impedance and junction temperature can be reduced by increasing the thermal area. The thermal area can be increased by adding metal heat dissipators to the leads of the diodes. Also, the shorter the distance between the diode and the heat sink or outside surface of the package, the lower the thermal impedance. In high-voltage applications, the minimum distance between the diode and outside surfaces will depend on the voltage stress of the package and on the dielectric strength of the potting material used.

CORONA
Corona is the result of ionization of gas (air, oxygen, etc.) that is caused by a high-voltage field. This extremely destructive phenomenon usually results in slow degradation of insulation materials that can result in latent failures. Careful design, consistent manufacturing processes, eliminating air entrapment in encapsulation, and thorough understanding of causes of corona are required to minimize this problem.

Application Information

High-Voltage Rectifiers

High-voltage is a relative term and warnings are similar whether applied to 100 volts or 100 kilovolts.

Applications include:
- X-Ray supplies
- Cathode-ray tube (CRT) supplies
- Microwave traveling-wave tube (TWT) supplies.

Bridges

Bridges are AC to DC power conversion devices comprised only of diodes. They are available in single and three-phase AC inputs and are used in all types of products that require a DC power source from an AC power source.

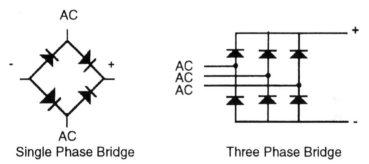

Single Phase Bridge   Three Phase Bridge

User must determine:
- Current surge (max.).
- Transient voltage (max.).
- DC output voltage and output current.
- Application thermal dissipation capability.
- AC peak input voltage and input frequency.
- AC voltage wave shape and current wave shape.
- Rectifier assembly heat dissipation and package size.
- Evaluate application environment extremes (i.e., temperature, altitude, and humidity).

Multipliers

Voltage multipliers are AC to DC power conversion devices. Multipliers are comprised of diodes and capacitors that can produce a high-potential DC output voltage (150KV) from a lower AC voltage source.

Applications include:
- CRT's
- Lasers
- X-Ray
- Copy machines
- Electrostatic systems
- 60 Hz power supplies
- Ion generators/pumps
- Portable power supplies
- High current power supplies.

The most common multiplier circuit is the Half-Wave Series multiplier.

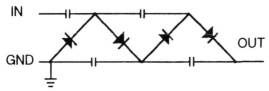

One stage is comprised of one diode and one capacitor. The above multiplier has four stages (referred to as a 4X circuit). There is uniform stress per stage on the diodes and capacitors. A wide range of multiplication stages can be joined together. Variations are listed below:
- Number of stages (odd or even) is unlimited, however, the regulation is proportional which makes an extremely large number of stages ineffective.
- Negative output voltage is produced by reversing the polarity of the diodes.
- Dual polarity output voltage is produced by connecting positive and negative multipliers together.
- Voltage may be tapped at any point on the filter bank of the capacitors.
- Any capacitor can be eliminated on the filter bank of the capacitors if the load is capacitive.

The following operating parameters must be taken into consideration:
- Ripple voltage
- Leakage currents
- Stray capacitance
- Regulation voltage.

Regulation voltage

Regulation is the drop in DC output voltage from the ideal voltage at a specified DC output current (assuming AC input voltage and frequency are constant).

Note: Regulation voltage is not to be confused with power losses dissipated in a multiplier. Power losses are primarily forward voltage losses in the diodes and rarely result in excessive multiplier temperatures.

Ripple voltage

Ripple voltage is the magnitude of fluctuation in DC output voltage at a specific output current (assuming AC input voltage and frequency are constant).

Stray capacitance

Stray capacitance becomes an important consideration as input frequency increases. Power losses through insulation which are negligible at 50/60Hz become significant at a high frequency.

Leakage currents

Losses due to leakage in diodes, capacitors, and insulation are significant considerations in applications that use very low capacitor values (i.e., night vision power supplies) and in applications that operate at high temperatures (>125°C).

Multiplier design steps that must be determined:
- Package size
- AC input voltage
- AC input frequency
- Operating DC output power
- Operating DC output voltage
- Evaluate application environment extremes (i.e., temperature, altitude, and humidity).

PARALLEL MULTIPLIERS
The theory of operation is the same for both series and parallel types. Parallel multipliers require less capacitance per stage, but require higher voltage rating on each successive stage. The net result is similar package volume but slightly different package shape capabilities. The limit on output voltage in parallel multipliers is determined by the voltage capability of capacitors (common single-layer ceramic capacitors do not exceed 20KV). Parallel multipliers tend to be convenient to add as output filters (RC) when the application requires extremely low ripple voltage.

Half-Wave Parallel Multiplier

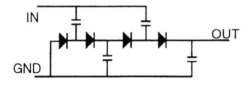

MULTIPLIER CIRCUIT COMPARISON

HALF-WAVE SERIES MULTIPLIER
- Low cost
- Very versatile
- Most common circuit
- Wide range of multiplication stages
- Uniform stress per stage on diodes and capacitors.

HALF-WAVE PARALLEL MULTIPLIER
- Small size
- Highly efficient
- Uniform stress on diodes
- Increasing voltage stress on capacitors with successive stages.

FULL-WAVE QUADRUPLER
- Good regulation
- Uniform diode stress
- Input capacitors only stressed at peak voltage.

FULL-WAVE MULTIPLIER
- High power capability
- Uniform component stress
- Wide range of multiplication stages.

FULL-WAVE SERIES-PARALLEL MULTIPLIER
- Uniform stress
- Highly efficient
- High power capability
- Increasing voltage stress on capacitors with successive stages.

Basic Circuits

Half-wave rectifier circuit.

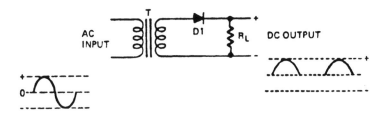

Full-wave rectifier circuit.

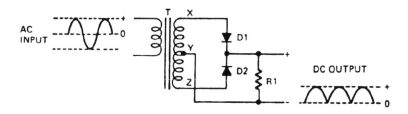

Full-wave bridge rectifier circuit.

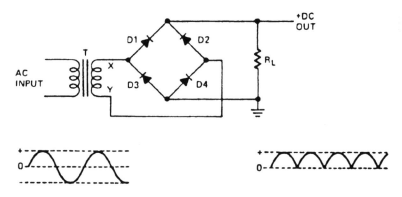

Simple capacitance filter circuit.

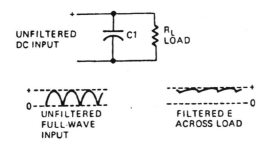

Chapter 3

LEDs and OPTOs

Before the development of the Light Emitting Diode (LED), there were two choices for status indication: neon and incandescent lamps. Both remain choices today, but are rapidly being replaced by LEDs.

The performance of LEDs has advanced to keep pace with the explosion of electronics technology into virtually every area of our lives. As LED efficiency increases, they are replacing neon and incandescent lamps in more and more applications. While using LEDs may seem simple enough, as with all electronic devices there are considerations you must understand to reap the highest levels of performance in every application. Careful consideration of these guidelines can make the difference between an acceptable indication solution and one that truly shines. In addition, there are more indicator mounting choices than ever before, including the widely-used surface-mount process. LEDs are becoming widely accepted in many applications where the incandescent lamp has been king. LEDs are even finding uses in large indicator applications ranging from vehicle brake lights to outdoor signs, in which an LED array can deliver unmatched long-term reliability, outstanding brightness, low power consumption, shock and vibration resistance, and no need for maintenance.

To simplify your optical design decisions, this chapter begins with a practical discussion of LEDs and their operation and applications, and continues with discussions of the major LED solutions available today. Covered are the basic characteristics of LEDs, how they compare with incandescent and neon lamps, LED packages and configurations, surface-mount devices, right-angle solutions, and panel mount indicators. You won't find any equations; this is a practical treatment of this subject.

LED FUNDAMENTALS

Light-emitting diodes (LEDs) are a reliable means of indication compared to light sources such as incandescent and neon lamps. LEDs are solid-state devices requiring little power and generating little heat. Because their heat generation is low and because they do not rely on a deteriorating material to generate light, LEDs have long operating lifetimes. One of the alternatives, incandescent bulbs, consume much more power, generate a great deal of heat, and rely on a filament that deteriorates in use. Neon bulbs, on the other hand, rely on an excited plasma which, along with its electrodes, can deteriorate over time. Both neon and many incandescent bulbs operate on AC line voltages, while LEDs operate from low-voltage, low-current DC lines.

The venerable incandescent bulb has been the predominant light source of choice in indication applications since there were things to indicate. It consists of a heated metal filament that radiates light inside a glass bulb. The radiated light is white, consisting of a wide spectrum of electromagnetic radiation. Incandescent bulbs generate high-intensity light for a short operating lifetime, and are susceptible to damage from vibration.

Neon bulbs consist of electrodes encased in a glass bulb with a phosphorescent gas. They offer relatively long operating lifetimes (compared to incandescent bulbs) with lower power consumption and better resistance to shock and vibration. However, they must run at a relative high-voltage AC and incorporate a current-limiting resistor. The light these lamps provide spans a relatively narrow portion of the color spectrum and is weak in comparison to incandescent bulbs and the brightest LEDs.

LEDs have extremely long operating lifetimes, low current draw from DC voltage lines, low heat dissipation, tremendous resistance to shock and vibration, and generally a smaller size than neon and incandescent bulbs. In addition, LEDs can be pulsed at very high switching speeds, and can be made to turn on and off with logic-level voltage signals. To be fair however, LEDs produce nearly monochromatic light (a single-color) and they have relatively narrow viewing ranges. Still, for a growing number of applications, LEDs provide an extremely effective solution.

LED Technology

LEDs are available in both visible colors and infrared. The visible colors include blue, yellow, green, and red, and fall into the spectral wavelength region from 400 to 700 nanometers (nm).

ELECTROMAGNETIC SPECTRUM

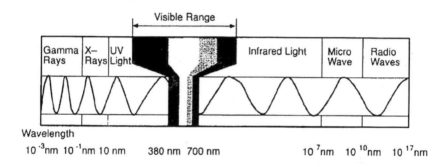

The human eye is most sensitive to green light at a wavelength of 563 nm. Bicolor LEDs are manufactured by combining two different LED chips within a common LED housing. Positive and negative voltages are applied to turn on either LED. Infrared LEDs, commonly used in remote controls for televisions and a wide variety of sensing and data communications applications, reach wavelengths of 940 nm and higher. The color of LEDs is determined exclusively by the semiconductor compound used to make it, not by the color of the surrounding epoxy lens. The lens color is used only to show in the "off" state what color the indicator will display when it is "on."

For most of the period since the LED was first introduced in 1969, red LEDs were by far the most efficient and produced the greatest light output. However, research by companies have produced significant advances in the efficiency of blue, green, and yellow LEDs. Today, yellow LEDs match the performance of red LEDs. These advances have great importance for the application of LEDs, and the greater their efficiency becomes, the more applications they can serve that have traditionally been served exclusively by incandescent lamps.

For example, the automotive industry wants to eliminate the incandescent bulb from as many places as possible; in the dashboard, for turn signals, and for brake lights. Current models from most automakers today use LEDs in the high-mounted center brake light, and work is being conducted to gain acceptance of LEDs in standard brake lights as well. The increase in efficiency of yellow LEDs now puts them in contention for use in turn signals as well.

LEDs have significant benefits in these automotive applications. In brake lights, turn signals, and in-dash indicators, the devices should never need to be replaced throughout the life of the car. For in-dash applications, this is an even more appealing virtue because removing the dashboard in todays automobiles is a difficult, time-consuming, and expensive procedure.

The automotive industry is just one example of a high-volume marketplace that is becoming accessible to the LED. Other transportation applications, as well as many others, will move from incandescent lamp to LED.

Operating Principles
How do LEDs emit light? The process is based on the change in energy levels when holes and electrons combine in the negative (N) region of a positive-negative (PN) semiconductor diode. During these shifts in energy, photons are generated, some of which are absorbed by the semiconductor material and some of which are emitted as light energy. The wavelength of the light depends on the difference of energy levels in the recombination process as well as the type of semiconductor material used to form the LED chip.

Most diodes are specified for spectral characteristics at a room temperature of 25°C. Although an LED's wavelength will shift with temperature, following a typical shift of about 0.1 to 0.3 nm/°C as temperature increases past room temperature, this color shift is not noticeable in most applications.

Brightness and Efficiency

An LED's brightness or luminous intensity is dependent upon the amount of forward bias current applied to the diode. An LED specified for a certain intensity with a 20mA current will provide about half intensity at 10mA. Luminous intensity is usually characterized in terms of millicandelas (mcd). A candela (1,000 mcd) is a unit of luminous intensity. Most LED manufacturers provide data sheets with minimum and typical values of luminous intensity.

An LED's quantum efficiency is based on the amount of light energy generated as a function of the amount of energy applied to the LED. At elevated temperatures, an LED's quantum efficiency decreases. It also decreases with age.

LEDs do not emit light uniformly in all directions, with a sharp drop in luminous intensity as a viewer moves away from a direct or on-axis vantage point. The half-intensity beam angle, given in degrees, is used to characterize how far in degrees from the on-axis perspective a particular LED's luminous intensity drops to 50 percent. For example, given two LEDs with equal luminous intensity, the LED with a half-intensity beam angle of 40° provides a wider viewing angle than the LED with a half-intensity beam angle of only 20°. This is true even though both may generate the same amount of luminous intensity for a given supply current.

Factors that contribute to viewing angle include the level of diffusant, the shape of the reflector cup which surrounds the LED chip, the shape of the LED lens, and the distance from the LED to the nose of the lens. When there is no diffusant, the viewing angle is ±10° to 12°; it can be up to ±70° when the maximum amount of diffusant is employed.

LED power dissipation is computed by multiplying the forward voltage by the forward current. For a typical LED with 2V forward voltage that is drawing 5mA current, the power dissipation is 10mW. Power dissipation is a key LED characteristic because it causes the temperature of the LED to increase. Light intensity decreases and wavelength increases with increasing temperature. Low power dissipation not only translates into cost-effective operation, but long operating lifetimes as well.

The amount of current drawn by the LED makes an enormous difference when arrays of LEDs are used. Increased efficiency delivers either more light for a given current or the same amount of light for less current. Incremental increases in efficiency may seem insignificant, but each advancement can open the door to another application that was previously served only by an incandescent lamp. While each LED does not draw much current, 50 LEDs in an array can draw a significant amount of current. For example, typical high efficiency LEDs once routinely drew 10mA from a 2VDC source. If 100 of these devices were used, 1.0A would be drawn. In some types of battery-operated equipment, this would be more current than the entire unit would be expected to draw. However, today's devices often draw 1 to 2mA, which means that in this hypothetical application the LED array would draw far less current from the battery.

Reliability data for different LEDs must be compared in terms of the amount of forward current that drives a particular LED. An LED may provide greater luminous intensity at higher current levels, but tends to have a shorter operating life-time compared to a device running at lower current levels. At higher current levels, LEDs also tend to more quickly lose total output power over time. At forward current levels of 20mA or less, LEDs are expected to last well over 100,000 hours, (more than 10 years.).

Secondary Optics
In addition to the LED itself, some applications require the use of secondary optics to carry the light from the LED to the desired location on the equipment. The most common type of secondary optics employs light pipes. As their name implies, light pipes simply provide a method of transferring the light generated by the LED from one place to another. They can consist of fiber optics or molded lenses that reflect the light and point it to the viewing location. In the manufacturing process, light pipes require the additional step of attachment to the circuit board or front panel. They are also made of materials that will not survive the surface-mount process temperatures.

Backlighting
Backlighting of front panel legends using LEDs is becoming extremely popular because it allows the panel to have a smooth and finished appearance and reduces manufacturing cost. In backlighting applications, the LEDs are located behind small translucent (usually Mylar) "windows" that are flush with the faceplate. The light from the LED illuminates the window.

Designers have sometimes used diffused LEDs for this purpose. This results in a lack of intensity in front of the window because diffused LEDs spread their output omnidirectionally and have a viewing angle of ±35°. Some of the intensity is dispersed and lost before it can arrive at the window.

In addition, a condition called crosstalk or light bleeding occurs between adjacent diffused LEDs because they are designed to spread (diffuse) the light they produce. Crosstalk also occurs with nondiffused LEDs but to a much lesser degree because their light is focused on the window and its intensity is greater there. Crosstalk makes an unlit LED appear to be "on" because light from an adjacent LED is transmitted through its lens to the front panel. Crosstalk also reduces the amount of light that reaches the front panel.

To solve this problem for designers, manufacturers have developed a family of right-angle housings that completely enshroud a high-intensity nondiffused LED. The combination of the LED and the housing results in zero crosstalk as well as an extremely bright on-axis indicator. It provides these attributes with much greater repeatability and ease of implementation than any other method.

LED Types

Regardless of the electrical characteristics, the designer basically has a choice of LEDs with a narrow viewing angle or a wide viewing angle. The LED is available with a wide variety of physical and optical characteristics. The basic LED consists of a diode chip or die, mounted in the coined reflector cup of a lead frame, wire bonded and encased in a solid epoxy lens. The lens may have particles of glass called diffusant, and it may be tinted as well. These characteristics can be combined to produce tinted-diffused, nontinted diffused (used with bicolor LEDs), and tinted-nondiffused LEDs, as well as "water clear" LEDs that have no tint or diffusion.

There are a variety of other options as well, including lens shape and size and the distance from the LED to the nose of the lens. When the LED is positioned near the nose of the lens, the widest possible viewing angle is produced (along with some sacrifice in on-axis luminous intensity). When it is positioned far back from the nose, the most narrow viewing angle is produced.

Diffused types have tiny glass particles in the epoxy lens. This spreads the light to a viewing angle of about ±35° from center. They are recommended for use in direct viewing applications in which the LED protrudes through a hole in the front panel of the equipment.

Nondiffused types without glass particles in the epoxy produce a narrow viewing angle of ±12°. They are often used for backlighting applications in which the LED light is focused on a translucent window in the front panel.

Tinted types for indication in the "off" state of what it's color will be when in the "on" state.

Water-clear (nontinted, nondiffused) types have no tint or diffusion in the epoxy and produce the greatest light output and narrowest viewing angle. They are designed for applications in which very high intensity or colorless LEDs in the "off-state" are desired.

Integral resistor types includes the resistor chip required for current limiting inside the package.

Low current types employ special diodes that draw the least amount of current from the power source (e.g., 2 mA).

Although LEDs are available in a wide range of shapes and sizes, three popular types are used most often:
- 2 mm (T - 3/4) LEDs
- 3 mm (T-1) LEDs
- 5 mm (T- 1 3/4) LEDs.

Basic types of LED mounting configurations:
- Cast epoxy through-hole LEDs designed for printed circuit board mounting. They are the most common type of LED in use.
- LEDs in a housing designed to deliver light at a right angle from the circuit board.
- LEDs in a right-angle surface mount compatible package employ a lens structure to direct the light.
- Surface-mountable discrete LEDs compatible with tape-and-reel automated assembly equipment for high-volume production.

Discrete LED vs. Packaged Solutions

Designers use LEDs in two basic applications; either as a diagnostic indicator on a circuit board inside a piece of equipment or for front panel status indication. Both applications can be served by either discrete LEDs or by packaged solutions that combines an LED with a plastic housing. While discrete LEDs may appear to have an advantage in cost, when the total installed cost of the device is considered, the packaged solution is generally less expensive.

Diagnostic applications do not require the same level of attention to esthetics as front panel applications, since the LED is generally viewed by a technician and is not designed to enhance the appearance of the equipment. However, the devices must still deliver consistent brightness and be positioned to ensure that the proper indicator is read. A key design goal in diagnostic applications is achieving maximum component density, so 2mm LEDs with an integral current-limiting resistor are employed to conserve circuit board space, which also reduces parts count. The LED is not viewed in bright light so there is no need for a high-intensity device.

Front panel applications require the same attention to component density, with increased emphasis on esthetic appeal. The LEDs must not only provide the basic indication or illumination function, they must also complement the appearance of the host equipment, since they are located on the front panel for all to see. In many cases, the appearance of the LEDs is actually a selling feature of the end product. Consequently, uniform color, alignment, and intensity are important considerations.

Discrete LEDs provide only a light source and leave the details of configuration, mounting, polarity, and alignment to the end user. For right angle applications, the manufacturer of the product must perform the steps of lead bending and alignment. For top-view applications, a means of assuring consistent LED height from the circuit board must be developed.

Discrete LEDs provide an acceptable solution if the designer wishes to perform the steps of lead trimming, bending, and alignment in-house. However, these steps require considerable labor and decrease throughput of the manufacturing process, adding cost to the end product. The packaged approach eliminates all of the steps in the manufacturing of a component into the board. When a multiple-LED component is used, it reduces the number of insertions per LED as well. The packaged approach reduces installed cost by lowering the overall manufacturing and labor costs, and by increasing throughput. It also simplifies the work required to specify, purchase, and track the indicator components.

Packaged LEDs have many other advantages. When discrete LEDs are used in right-angle applications, misalignment with the front panel can occur. If the LED must protrude through a hole in the panel, additional steps may be necessary including hand soldering after bending the leads to manually align each LED with the panel. With the packaged solution, LED height and alignment are consistent, because the LED is encased in a precision molded housing.

The housing maintains proper alignment of both the LED and its leads, and provides stability and ensures higher reliability. Contrast ratio is increased because the LEDs are encased in black plastic, and many types include integral standoffs, which prevent flux entrapment and aid circuit board cleaning. Packaged LED components also incorporate LEDs that are matched in both intensity and color, which ensures a uniform appearance, and eliminates the need for the customer to sort and measure the intensity of the devices.

A packaged approach provides an esthetic solution at the lowest possible installed cost.

Surface-Mount LEDs

Since the mid-1980s, surface mounting of electronic components has become more and more widespread. Today it is almost universally utilized throughout the electronics industry because it increases the throughput of the manufacturing process, reduces direct labor, eliminates multiple component attachment techniques, allows the use of smaller PC boards and greater component density, and increases product reliability.

There are very few traditional electronic components that research and development efforts have not been able to make surface mountable. Most of the holdouts are either oddly shaped, sensitive to high heat or handling, or are in some way incompatible with pick-and-place robotic systems.

However, every year more and more of these holdouts are converted to surface-mount compatibility.

The LED was one of these holdouts, but today there are surface-mount LED solutions that satisfy the requirements of any application, from simple diagnostic environments to horizontal and vertical stacks and right-angle packages for front panel viewing.

It is important to point out that the obstacles created by the surface-mount environment have been surmounted only through considerable research and development. The requirements of surface mounting are nearly all detrimental to achieving good optical performance. In general, a broad range of focal depth is desirable, along with the ability to use a reflector cup and a rounded lens. The surface-mount process makes all of these attributes either difficult or impossible to achieve.

For example, surface-mount LEDs must be lightweight in order to be picked up by the suction of vacuum pick-and-place equipment. This severely reduces the amount of optics that can be incorporated in the device. The devices must also be flat, which both hinders optical performance and reduces the number of options available to the designer. Surface-mount LEDs must also be small enough to fit in EIA-standard tape-and-reel packaging. The package must be self-aligning and able to withstand the high reflow temperatures and harsh solvents encountered in the surface-mount environment. Finally, the optics and esthetic features of the device must survive the process unscathed.

In the short time that surface-mount LEDs have been available, manufacturers have made great progress in bringing the traditional characteristics of the through-hole LED to the surface-mount environment.

In the early 1980s the first LEDs constructed of materials that could survive the surface mount process were introduced. These devices, configured in the familiar SOT-23 transistor package, allowed LEDs to be robotically placed on the circuit board for the first time.

As a way to incorporate optics with the device and to broaden the number of options available, designers looked to standard cast-epoxy through-hole type LEDs, and pressed them into service as surface-mount components. In this operation, the leads of the device were bent, held in place, their leads soldered, and the final angle of the device (presumably around 90° from vertical) determined. The technique essentially negates the inherent advantages in throughput and cost provided by surface mounting. It has also proven to be unreliable because in repeated tests, through-hole LED's have been shown not to be process-survivable. Consequently, it is generally not employed today.

Current substrate and lead-frame type surface-mount LEDs were introduced in the mid 1980s to satisfy both the requirements of surface mounting and optical performance. However, LEDs alone do not address the need to direct light output from the circuit board to the front panel, which is a frequent requirement.

This need was addressed through development of a device called a light pipe, which acts as a conduit for the light, routing it from the LED to its intended viewing location. Light pipes are a viable solution in many situations, but add a manual manufacturing step (placement of the light pipe).

LED Construction types

Two different types of surface-mount LED constructions are available to the designer: substrate and lead-frame. Each one is optimized to reduce the stress on the die as it goes through the soldering process.

The advantage of the substrate type is its compact size, which makes it well suited for low-cost, high-density applications. Although standard substrate devices have traditionally had no optics, lenses are now being molded on the LED to provide some optical characteristics. Within the substrate category, there are two choices of material: ceramic and glass epoxy. Ceramic types are white, which reflects the light upward. They also withstand high temperatures and high current. Their disadvantages include poor low temperature performance below -20°C. Glass epoxy types are designed to withstand temperatures of -40°C, but they are the color of a printed circuit, and so do not reflect light as well as their ceramic counterparts. In either case, the LED die is bonded to terminals that are integrated or attached to the substrate.

In the lead-frame type, the lead frame is molded into a high-temperature plastic housing and the LED chip is bonded directly to the lead frame. This type has better optics because it allows for use of a reflector cup, which cannot be accommodated in the substrate type configuration. It is also more robust in construction. However, it is also larger.

Secondary Optics

Unlike their through-hole counterparts, which incorporate secondary optics such as a reflector, lens, and diffusant along with the die, surface-mount LEDs require these features to be added externally based on the needs of the application. The designer who chooses to use surface-mount LEDs must realize that the basic device is just a point source of light in a package designed for manufacturing compatibility, and that he or she must address the issue of providing secondary optics.

Secondary optics direct the light to the proper place, generally 90° from the perpendicular direction in which the device is mounted. In order to add secondary optics to the discrete surface-mount LED, the designer has two alternatives.

The first method is to place discrete surface-mount LEDs on the board and attach a component called a light pipe to the circuit board or front panel after the soldering process. The light pipe is a precision, molded plastic component that routes the light from the die to the intended viewing location at a right angle from the circuit board.

This approach has one primary disadvantage: it requires an assembly step to properly place the light pipe. However, it has significant advantages as well, they are:
- LED alignment is less critical.
- The viewing surface is changeable.
- The designer has flexibility in selecting a shape and size LED.
- Backlighting and direct view applications can be accommodated.
- There is good access to the surface-mount LED for rework and inspection.
- There is minimal interaction with the front panel, therefore, there is no burden on its design.

Light pipes are especially useful in applications requiring a horizontal or vertical array of LED indicators. With careful light pipe design, it is frequently possible to create a single molded part to redirect the light from multiple LEDs to multiple front-panel indicator positions without optical crosstalk between them. This can result in a low installed cost per indicator position.

The light pipe is a deceptively simple device. Since LEDs have a limited amount of light output, the light pipe must ensure that as much of this light as possible reaches the panel. This requires critical ray tracing to optimize the light pipe's optical transmission performance. In addition, the requirement for easy circuit-board mounting provides opportunities for light loss which must be addressed in the light pipe design.

Finally, molding techniques must be precise in order to minimize any impurities and air bubbles in the plastic along with inconsistencies inherent in the molding process.

The second method of applying secondary optics is to employ a fully process-compatible component containing both an LED light source and optics. This solution does not require post-process insertion of additional components on the circuit board, and the entire solution, including LED die, optics, and light pipe, can be placed on the board in a single assembly step. The disadvantages of this approach include a limitation on size and height, difficulty in inspecting the device and reworking its attachment, and higher cost.

Deciphering the Real Cost

From a cost standpoint, it sometimes appears less expensive to continue manufacturing mixed-technology circuit boards because the surface-mount component can be more expensive than its through-hole counterpart. However, the total installed cost can be less when using a surface-mount LED because it is much less labor-intensive to install and allows a higher component density to be achieved on the board. In addition, the designer has the ability to use both sides of the board. Making the move to surface-mount also reduces by one the types of components that must still be through-hole mounted, speeding the conversion to all surface-mount assembly.

Fortunately for the designer, there are an increasing number of LED indicator solutions available for surface mounting. The only decision is to choose the proper one for a given design.

Application Information

LED Lamps

Electronic instruments have undergone a striking improvement in reliability due to the increased use of solid state and integrated circuitry. As a result, increasingly higher reliability is demanded of the electronic components used in these instruments, and new products are being developed in rapid succession. As an electronic component, LEDs have proved themselves far superior to other display components in terms of luminance and life, and the development of LEDs with new shapes and improved performance is being pursued.

As a result, the conventional use of LEDs as pilot lights is being overshadowed by new applications in commercial electronics, including television channel displays and audio equipment displays. Uses in communications and outdoor displays are also increasing. LEDs are contributing to improved reliability in these devices.

LED Chips

In recent years dramatic reductions have been made in the size, thickness, and weight of portable telephones, video cassette recorders, and other electronic devices. This has created a rapidly increasing demand for surface-mount LED chips which permit reflow soldering. Chip LEDs are being used in a wide range of fields, particularly the communication device market.

Light pipes are used in surface-mount applications in which a discrete SMT LED is automatically placed on the PC board, and the emitted light needs to be displayed on the front panel of the equipment. The light pipe can be secured to the front panel by an ultrasonic welding process. The light is brought to the front panel once the product is assembled.

Each light pipe is designed to transmit the light of a specific LED, and its shape is defined by a CAD ray tracing program to optimize its light transmission efficiency. A properly designed light pipe will provide an optically efficient and aesthetically uniform solution.

Lights pipes are required when:
- Unique shapes for the indicators are needed.
- Arrays (rows and/or columns) of surface-mount indicators are required on the front panel.
- LEDs are located a distance from or are emitting light in a different direction from the front panel.
- Desired additional protection against electro-static discharge (ESD) as the LED is isolated by the polycarbonate light pipe material.

LED Displays

Typical examples of LED display applications include:
- Toys
- Car displays
- Deluxe cameras
- Medical equipment
- Industrial equipment
- Electrical decorations
- Household appliances
- Measuring instruments.

With improvements in LED emitter manufacturing technology, assembly technology and packaging technology, LEDs are responding to demands for the same level of reliability as other semiconductor products, and they are finding applications in an ever expanding range of fields. LEDs were first used on a wide scale commercial basis as monolithic numeric displays in clocks and calculators. GaAsP (Gallium, Arsenide, Phosphorus), GaAlAs (Gallium, Aluminum, Arsenide), GaP (Gallium, Phosphorus), and other emitting materials are being applied to uses suitable to their individual characteristics. Applications include direct-view LEDs, reflector LEDs, flat displays for illumination, and dot matrix units of sizes from 40 to 200 or more.

OPTOs

Optoelectronic sensor devices are comprised of emitters, detectors, and interrupters. An infrared LED is the emitter. A photodiode or phototransistor can be used as the detector. Sensors transmit light, therefore, the plastic used for them differs from the black molding materials used for transistors and other IC's in that an almost pure epoxy resin is used. This resin is slightly weaker than the black molding materials in terms of heat tolerance, resistance to chemicals, and mechanical strength. For these reasons, caution must be exercised when handling and mounting these devices.

Infrared LEDs

Infrared emitting diodes emit in the near infrared spectral range between 800nm and 1000nm. Infrared radiation is produced by radiative recombination of electrons and holes from the conduction and valence bands. The emitted photon energy corresponds closely to the bandgap energy. The internal efficiency depends on the band structure, the doping material, and the doping level. Direct bandgap materials offer high efficiencies because no photons are needed for recombination of electrons and holes. GaAs is a direct gap material and the mixed crystal, GaAlAs, (made from the pure compounds GaAs and AlAs) are the limited selection of materials. GaAlAs infrared chips are for higher output; approximately 1.3 to 1.5 times that of the GaAs chip.

The materials are formed by the liquid phase epitaxy (LPE) crystal growth method. This method uses Ga solutions containing As, possibly Al, and the doping substance. The solution is saturated at high temperature, typically 900°C, and GaAs substrates are dipped into the liquid. The solubility of As and Al decreases with decreasing temperature. In this way, epitaxial layers can be grown by slow cooling of the solution. Several layers differing in composition may be obtained using different solutions one after another as needed for doubled heterostructures which consist normally of two layers that confine a layer with a much smaller bandgap.

The life of semiconductors is often said to be limitless. However, this is not the case for infrared LEDs, as they lose output power. When designing circuitry for an infrared LED, design in sufficient margin to allow for the LED's life (loss of output power). Typical changes in output power as time elapses are shown in the manufacturer's data sheet. In cases where current will pass for prolonged periods of time, be sure to allow sufficient design margin so that the circuit will not malfunction if the output falls to the level of the maximum fall-off curve.

The chip housing structures of infrared LEDs can be divided into the three following types:

Can type
The chip is mounted on a metal stem and then covered with a windowed cap. A variety of different directivities can be obtained by varying the shape of the cap lens.

Cast type
The chip is mounted on a lead frame and then liquid resin is poured into the mold and allowed to harden.

Molded type
This type is packaged by transfer molding.

Infrared LED symbol

ANODE   CATHODE

Infrared LED applications:
- Optical control equipment
- Radiation source for sensors
- High speed data transmission
- Radiation source for remote control devices
- Transmission of audio signals between audio devices
- Transmission of images from a video cassette recorder to a TV.

Photodiodes

When light shines on a silicon PN junction, the light will cause the formation of electron and hole pairs in the silicon crystal. If the energy of the light is greater that the silicon energy bandgap, the electrons and holes will diffuse according to the concentration gradient of the PN junction, with electrons flowing into the N layer and holes flowing into the P layer. Thus by connecting an external load, current will flow from the N layer to the P layer, which is the reverse direction of the PN junction. PN and PIN are two types of photodiodes. Photodiodes are generally housed in a can type, ceramic stem type, or molded type packages.

Photodiode Symbol

ANODE   CATHODE

Phototransistors

A phototransistor can be thought of as a photodiode connected to a silicon planar transistor. The principle of operation is essentially amplification by an NPN transistor of photo current generated by light irradiation. Phototransistors consist of a single type and a Darlington type. In the Darlington type, the current is further amplified by another transistor and the output current is greater than the single type. However, a drawback of this is a slower response speed. Phototransistors are housed in a can type, cast type, or molded type enclosures.

Phototransistor applications:
- Light source for sensors
- Optical control equipment.

Phototransistor symbol

Darlington circuit schematic

Photo ICs

Photo IC is a detector with a digital output. When irradiated by light, one type has high transistor output and another type has low output. Both types can be directly connected to TTL, CMOS, and other logic circuits with the advantages of easy circuit design, space conservation, and low cost. A photo IC is an integration of a photodiode, constant voltage circuit, Schmitt trigger, and other elements into a single chip using bipolar IC technology.

Common packages have three leads and are normally molded.

Photointerrupters

Photointerrupters are multi-element devices and are also called transparent photosensors, which consist of an emitter and a detector facing each other. Detection occurs when an object interrupts the light beam passing from the emitter to the detector. The emitter is a high-output GaAs infrared LED with long life, and the detector is normally a single phototransistor or a Darlington phototransistor.

Interrupters are generally housed in case-insertion packages or single-chip molded packages. Case-insertion types are most commonly used and consist of an emitter and detector inserted in an injection molded case. The single-chip molded package responds to recent needs for increasingly compact devices. The molding is carried out by injection which makes it easy to achieve a compact package.

Photointerrupter applications:
- Printers
- Cameras
- Facsimiles
- Optical switches
- Movie equipment
- Floppy disk drives
- Plain paper copiers
- Optical control equipment.

Photointerrupter symbol

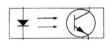

Photoreflectors

Photoreflectors, also a multi-element device, are reflective-type photosensors consisting of an emitter and a detector facing the same direction. As light reflected from an object is detected, the output level is generally low and thus a single silicon phototransistor is used together with a Darlington transistor for the detector.

Photoreflective applications:
- Copiers
- Game machines
- Compact disc players
- Office automation equipment.

Photoreflector symbol

Photo IC interrupters

Photo IC interrupters essentially take the output of a phototransistor (single or Darlington) and converts it to a photo IC output. The output is digital with one type being *high* and another type being *low* when irradiated with light.

Remote control sensors

Remote control detector ICs integrate a photodiode and a signal processing circuit into a single chip using bipolar IC technology. These devices may be electromagnetically shielded by aluminum wiring and therefore require no external shielding.

The most common application is in consumer electronic products.

Optocouplers

Optocouplers are designed for use in analog or digital interface applications that require high-voltage isolation between the input and output. The basic optocoupler channel consist of a LED source which is optically coupled to a silicon phototransistor. There are choices of numerous channels in one package.

Optocoupler diagram

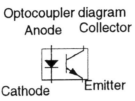

Applications:
- Industrial robots
- Sequence controllers
- I/O interfaces for computers
- Telephone sets, telephone exchanges
- System appliances, measuring instruments
- Electric home appliances such as fan heaters
- Registers, copiers, automatic vending machines
- Medical instruments, physical and chemical equipments
- Signal transmission between circuits of different potentials and impedances.

Laser Diodes

The market for compact discs, video discs, and optical memory used as optical disc files has been expanding rapidly. In addition, the demand for laser beam printers in the office automation market has been growing dramatically. All of these products use AlGaAs (Aluminum, Gallium, Arsenide) laser diodes for their light source with a wavelength from 785nm to 850nm. Laser diodes are normally made by a liquid layer growth method called liquid phase epitaxy. However, laser diodes can also be made by molecular beam epitaxy (MBE), which allows precise control of composition and layer thickness. Laser diodes (semiconductor lasers) have a much longer life than other lasers such as gas or solid-state lasers.

Laser Diode applications:

Audio / Visual
- Sights
- Pointers
- CD-ROM Drives
- Mini Disc Players
- Laser Disc Players
- Video Disc Players
- Compact Disc Players.

Office Automation Equipment
- Pointers
- Sensors
- Laser fax
- CD-ROM
- Bar code readers
- Laser beam printers
- Measuring instruments.

Information Processing Equipment
- Phase change discs
- Optical disc memory.

Communication Equipment
- Optical LAN
- Data transmission
- Atmospheric transmission.

Fundamental Characteristics

Optical output vs. forward current
This is the most fundamental characteristic of a laser diode. As the temperature rises, the threshold current and operating current increase.

Emission spectrum
The emission spectrum of a laser (longitudinal mode) is an important characteristic when actually using the laser. Before using a laser, consideration must be given to the dependence of the wavelength on temperature and the dependence of the emission spectrum on optical output.

Far-field pattern
In addition to the longitudinal mode, lasers have a transverse mode. The optical intensity distribution of the transverse mode appearing at the laser facet is called the near-field pattern, and the optical intensity distribution at a sufficient distance from the facet is called the far-field pattern. Due to its stable single transverse mode, there are no deviations of peak points or variations in the optical intensity distribution when operating within rated values.

Precautions

Absolute maximum ratings
If an excessively large current flows in a laser diode, a large optical output will occur and the emitting facet may sustain damage. This optical damage can occur even with momentary over-current. For this reason, absolute maximum ratings which must not be exceeded even momentarily have been established. Exercise particular caution with respect to the drive voltage supply and static electricity. These ratings are established for a case temperature of 25°C. As the temperature of a laser diode increases, its maximum output will decrease and the operating range will shrink. Even when operated within the absolute maximum ratings, operation at high temperature will result in a shorter life than operation at low temperature. For this reason, the design should include sufficient margin for heat radiation and light output.

Heat radiation conditions

Like other semiconductors, prolonged operation of a laser diode will cause heat to build up at junctions and increased case temperature. For this reason, attach aluminum (or other) heat sinks to the stem of the laser.

Protection against electrostatic discharge and other current surges

Electro-static discharge and other current surges can cause deterioration and damage in laser diodes, resulting in reduced reliability. Take the following protective measures:

- Ground the device and circuits. Install surge filters, surge reduction transformers, or other electro-static discharge protectors in the power supply inputs.
- When working with laser diodes, wear anti-static clothing including footwear and caps. Grounded wrist straps should always be worn while working with laser diodes, and the strap should be grounded through a $1M\Omega$ resistance.
- Use anti-static containers for transport and storage.
- Laser deterioration and damage can occur due to excessive current spikes when the power is turned on or off. Design circuits to avoid the generation of excessive current spikes.
- Inductive surges near equipment that emits high-frequency EMI can damage or destroy lasers. Avoid using lasers near fluorescent lamps or other sources of EMI emissions.

Soldering

Use a grounded soldering iron to solder laser leads. Solder at a temperature of no more than 250°C for a maximum of 3 seconds, at a point at least 2mm from the base of the leads. Some diodes recommend 1mm.

Handling laser diodes

Never touch the glass window of the laser. A damaged or dirtied window will impair the performance of the laser.

Handling packages

Due to the glass window in each device, packages must not be dropped or subjected to excessive pressure.

Safety

It is extremely dangerous to look, either directly or through a lens, at the laser beam emitted from a laser diode. Use a TV camera or other similar device to adjust the optical axis.

The laser beam emitted from a laser diode may be invisible to the human eye, however, it will injure the eye and sufficient caution must be exercised to avoid direct exposure or exposure through a fiber to the beam when a laser diode is in operation. Safety standards governing laser radiation include the U.S. standards (ANSIZ136.1) drafted and enacted in 1973, the IEC standards (IEC Publication 825) established in 1988, and Japan's JIS standards (JIS C6802) established in 1988. To protect the user from injury due to laser beam exposure, the standards consist of requirements both for the device and for the user.

The laser beam of a Class IIIb device must not be viewed directly and the device must not be touched. Furthermore, equipment in which these devices are incorporated must include interlocks and other safety features. To adjust the optical axis or performance and other similar work, it is recommended to use an infrared-sensitive TV camera along with wearing protective glasses.

Glossary

Semiconductor Definitions

Absolute maximum ratings

The values specified for "ratings," "maximum ratings," or "absolute maximum ratings" are based on the "absolute system" and unless otherwise required for a specific test method are not to be exceeded under any service or test conditions. These ratings are limiting values beyond which the serviceability of any individual semiconductor device may be impaired. Unless otherwise specified, the voltage, current, and power ratings are based on continuous DC power conditions at free air ambient temperature of +25°C. For pulsed or other conditions of operation of similar nature, the current, voltage, and power dissipation ratings are a function of time and duty cycle. In order not to exceed absolute ratings, the equipment designer has the responsibility of determining an average design value, for each rating, below the absolute value of that rating by a safety factor, so that the absolute values will never be exceeded under any usual conditions of supply-voltage variation, load variation, or manufacturing variation in the equipment itself.

Ambient temperature

Ambient temperature is the air temperature measured below a semiconductor device, in an environment of substantially uniform temperature, cooled only by natural air convection and not materially affected by reflective and radiant surfaces.

Anode

The electrode from which the forward current flows within the device.

Blocking

A term describing the state of a semiconductor device or junction which eventually prevents the flow of current.

Breakdown voltage

The breakdown voltage is the maximum instantaneous voltage, including repetitive and nonrepetitive transients, which can be applied across a junction in the reverse direction without an external means (circuit) of limiting the current. It is also the instantaneous value of reverse voltage at which a transition commences from a region of high small-signal impedance to a region of substantially lower small-signal impedance.

Case mount

A type of package (outline) which provides a method of readily attaching one surface of the semiconductor device to a heat dissipater to achieve thermal management of the case temperature (examples: TO-3, DO-4, etc.).

Case temperature

Case temperature is that temperature measured at a specified point on the case of a semiconductor device.

Cathode

The electrode to which the forward current flows within the device.

Characteristic

An inherent and measurable property of a device. Such a property may be electrical, mechanical, thermal, hydraulic, electromagnetic, or nuclear, and can be expressed as a value for stated or recognized conditions. A characteristic may also be a set of related values usually shown in graphical form.

Constant current source

A current source shall be considered constant if halving the generator impedance does not produce a change in the parameter being measured that is greater than the required precision of the measurement.

Constant voltage source

A voltage source shall be considered constant if doubling the generator impedance does not produce a change in the parameter being measured that is greater than the required precision of the measurement.

Disc type

A type of package (outline) for very high power devices which provides two parallel surfaces for mounting into a specialized heat dissipator capable of applying a specified compressive force to the device.

Forward bias

The bias which tends to produce current flow in the forward direction (P-type semiconductor region at a positive potential relative to N-type region).

Impulse duration

The time required for an impulse waveform to decay to 50 percent of the peak value measured from the start of the virtual front duration of zero crossover.

Impulse waveform

A pulse with a defined virtual front and impulse duration for either a voltage or current amplitude of unidirectional polarity.

Noise figure

At a selected input frequency, the noise figure is the *ratio* of the total noise power per unit bandwidth (at a corresponding output frequency) delivered to the output termination; *to* the portion thereof contributed at the input frequency by the input termination whose noise temperature is standard (293°K) at all frequencies.

Open circuit

A circuit shall be considered as open circuited if halving the magnitude of the terminating impedance does not produce a change in the parameter being measured greater than the specified accuracy of the measurement.

Package type

A package type is a package which has the same case outline, configuration, materials (including bonding, wire, or ribbon and die attach), piece parts (excluding preforms which differ only in size), and assembly processes.

Passivation

A grown oxide.

Pulse

A pulse is a flow of electrical energy of short duration.

Pulse average time

The average pulse time of a pulse is the time duration from a point on the leading edge which is 50 percent of the maximum amplitude to a point on the trailing edge which is 50 percent of the maximum amplitude.

Pulse delay time

The delay time of a pulse is the time interval from a point at which the leading edge of the input pulse has risen to 10 percent of its maximum amplitude to a point at which the leading edge of the output pulse has risen to 10 percent of its maximum amplitude.

Pulse fall time

The fall time of a pulse is that time duration during which the amplitude of its trailing edge is decreasing from 90 to 10 percent of the maximum amplitude.

Pulse rise time

The rise time of a pulse is that time duration during which the amplitude of its leading edge is increasing from 10 to 90 percent of the maximum amplitude.

Pulse storage time

The storage time of a pulse is the time interval from a point 10 percent down from the maximum amplitude on the trailing edge of the input pulse to a point 10 percent down from the maximum amplitude on the trailing edge of the output pulse.

Pulse time

The time of a pulse is the interval from the point on the leading edge which is 90 percent of the maximum amplitude *to* the point on the trailing edge which is 90 percent of the maximum amplitude.

Radiation failures

A radiation failure is defined at the lowest radiation level when either any device parameter exceeds its specified Post Irradiation Parameter Limits (PIPL) or the device fails any functional test in accordance with stated test conditions.

Radiation Hardness Assurance (RHA)

That portion of performance verification testing that assures that parts meet the radiation response characteristics as specified in this specification and the performance specification sheet.

Rating

The nominal value of any electrical, thermal, mechanical, or environmental quantity assigned to define the operating conditions under which a component, machine, apparatus, or electronic device is expected to give satisfactory service.

Reverse bias

The bias which tends to produce current flow in the reverse direction (N-type semiconductor region at a positive potential relative to the P-type region).

Semiconductor devices

Electronic device in which the characteristic distinguishing electronic conduction takes place within a semiconductor.

Semiconductor diode

A semiconductor device having two terminals and exhibiting a nonlinear voltage-current characteristic.

Semiconductor junction

A region of transition between semiconductor regions of different electrical properties (e.g., N-N+, PN, P-P+ semiconductors) or between a metal and a semiconductor.

Short circuit

A circuit shall be considered short-circuited if doubling the magnitude of the terminating impedance does not produce a change in the parameter being measured that is greater than the specified accuracy of the measurement.

Small signal

A signal shall be considered small if doubling its magnitude does not produce a change in the parameter being measured that is greater than the specified accuracy of the measurement.

Storage temperature
Storage temperature is a temperature at which the device may be stored without any power being applied.

Temperature coefficient
The ratio of the change in a parameter to the change in temperature.

Thermal compression bond
A bond achieved when pressure and temperature are present regardless of how the temperature rise was achieved except without ultrasonic assist.

Thermal equilibrium
Thermal equilibrium is reached when doubling the test time interval does not produce a change, due to thermal effects, in the parameter being measured that is greater than the specified accuracy of the measurement.

Thermal resistance
Thermal resistance is the temperature rise, per unit power dissipation, of a junction above the temperature of a stated external reference point under conditions of thermal equilibrium.

Thyristor
A bistable semiconductor device that comprises three or more junctions and can be switched from the "off" state or "on" state to the opposite state.

Transistor
An active semiconductor device capable of providing power amplification and having three or more terminals.

Virtual front duration
The pulse time as defined by 1.67 times time for voltage to increase from 30 percent to 90 percent of crest (peak value) or 1.25 times time for current to increase from 10 percent to 90 percent of crest.

Semiconductor symbols

F .... Noise figure

R_θ .... Thermal resistance

$R_{\theta CA}$ .... Thermal resistance, case to ambient

$R_{\theta JA}$ .... Thermal resistance, junction to ambient

$R_{\theta JC}$ .... Thermal resistance, junction to case

$R_{\theta JL}$ .... Thermal resistance, junction to lead

$R_{\theta JR}$ .... Thermal resistance, junction to reference

T_A .... Ambient or free air temperature

T_C .... Case temperature

TEC .... End cap temperature

T_j .... Junction temperature

TL .... Lead temperature

T_{op} .... Operating temperature

T_{STG} .... Storage temperature

t_d .... Delay time

t_f .... Fall time

t_{off} .... Turn-off time

t_{on} .... Turn-on time

t_p .... Pulse time

t_r .... Rise time

t_s .... Storage time

t_w .... Pulse average time

$V_{(BR)}$ .... Breakdown voltage

Note: Symbology may vary amoung manufacturers. The symbols used in this section are listed in the military standard for the general performance specifications of semiconductor devices (Mil-Prf 19500L).

Signal diode and Rectifier diode definitions

Semiconductor rectifier diode
A device having an asymmetrical voltage-current characteristic used for rectification.

Semiconductor signal diode
A device having an asymmetrical voltage-current characteristic used for signal detection.

Diode and Rectifier symbols

C_J .... Junction capacitance

$I_{F(RMS)}$, I_f, I_F, $I_{F(AV)}$, i_F, I_F .... Forward current

I_{FSM} .... Forward current, surge peak

$I_{F(OV)}$ .... Forward current, overload

I_O .... Average forward current, 180" conduction angle, 60 Hz, half sine wave

$I_{R(RMS)}$, I_r, I_R, $I_{R(AV)}$, i_R, I_{RM} .. Reverse current

$I_{R(REC)}$, $I_{RM(REC)}$ .... Reverse recovery current

I_{RRM} .... Reverse current, repetitive peak

I_{RSM} Reverse .... Reverse current, surge peak

P_F, $P_{F(AV)}$, P_F, P_{FM} .... Forward power dissipation

P_R, $P_{R(AV)}$, P_R, P_{RM} .... Reverse power dissipation

Q_S .... Stored charge

t_{fr} .... Forward recovery time

t_{rr} .... Reverse recovery time

$V_{(BR)}, v_{(BR)}$ .... Breakdown voltage (DC, instantaneous total value)

$V_{F(RMS)}, V_f, V_F, V_{F(AV)}, v_F, V_{FM}$... Forward voltage

$V_{R(RMS)}, V_r, V_R, V_{r(AV)}, v_R, V_{RM}$ .... Reverse voltage

V_{RWM} .... Working peak reverse voltage

V_{RRM} .... Repetitive peak reverse voltage

V_{RSM} .... Nonrepetitive peak reverse voltage

LETTER SYMBOL TABLE FOR DIODES AND RECTIFIERS.

	Total RMS value	RMS value of alternating component	DC value NO alternating component	DC value WITH alternating component	Instanta-neous total value	Maximum (peak) total value
Forward current	$I_{F(RMS)}$	I_f	I_F	$I_{F(AV)}$	I_F	I_{FM}
Forward current, average, 180°C condition angle 60 hz, half sine wave				I_O		
Forward current repetitive peak						I_{FRM}
Forward current, surge peak						I_{FSM}
Forward current, overload						$I_{F(OV)}$
Reverse current	$I_{R(RMS)}$	I_r	I_R	$I_{R(AV)}$	i_R	I_{RM}
Reverse recovery current					$i_{R(REC)}$	$I_{RM(REC)}$
Forward power dissipation			P_F	$P_{F(A)}$	P_F	P_{FM}
Reverse power dissipation			P_R	$P_{R(A)}$	P_R	P_{RM}
Forward voltage	$V_{F(RMS)}$	V_f	V_F	$V_{F(A)}$	V_F	V_{FM}
Reverse voltage	$V_{R(RMS)}$	V_r	V_R	$V_{R(A)}$	V_R	V_{RM}

	Total RMS value	RMS value of alternating component	DC value NO alternating component	DC value WITH alternating component	Instanta-neous total value	Maximum (peak) total value
Reverse voltage working peak						V_{RWM}
Reverse voltage repetitive peak						V_{RRM}
Reverse voltage nonrepetitive peak						V_{RRM}
Breakdown voltage			$V_{(BR)}$		$V_{(BR)}$	

Current regulator diode definition

Current regulator diode
A diode which limits current to an essentially constant value over a specified voltage range.

Current regulator diode symbols

I_L .... Limiting current

I_P .... Regulator current

V_K .... Knee voltage

V_L .... Limiting voltage

AI_P .... Regulator current variation

V_S .... Regulator voltage

z_k .... Knee impedance

z_s .... Regulator impedance

α_{IP} .... Temperature coefficient of regulator current

Voltage regulator / Voltage reference diode definitions

Voltage reference / diode
A diode which is normally biased to operate in the breakdown region of its voltage-current characteristic and which develops across its terminals a reference voltage of specified accuracy, when biased to operate throughout a specified current and temperature range.

Voltage regulator diode

A diode which is normally biased to operate in the breakdown region of its voltage-current characteristic and which develops across its terminals an essentially constant voltage throughout a specified current range.

Voltage regulator and voltage reference diode symbols

I_F .... Forward current, DC

I_R .... Reverse current, DC

I_Z, I_{ZK}, I_{ZM}, I_{ZSM} .... Regulator current, reference current (DC, DC near breakdown knee, DC maximum rated current, DC maximum rated surge current)

V_F .... Forward voltage, DC

V_R .... Reverse voltage, DC

V_Z, V_{ZM} .... Regulator voltage, reference voltage (DC, DC at maximum rated current)

z_z, z_{zk}, z_{zm} .... Regulator impedance, reference impedance (small-signal, at I_Z, at I_{ZK}, at I_{ZM})

α_{VZ} .... Temperature coefficient of regulator voltage, temperature coefficient of reference voltage

Microwave diode definitions

Detector diode
A device which converts RF energy into DC or video output.

Gunn diode
A microwave diode that exhibits negative resistance arising from the bulk negative differential conductivity occurring in several compound semiconductors such as gallium arsenide (GaAs), and that operates at a frequency determined by the transit time of charge bunches formed by this negative differential conductivity.

IMPATT diode (IMPact, Avalanche, and Transit Time diode)
A semiconductor microwave diode that, when its junction is biased into avalanche, exhibits a negative resistance over a frequency range determined by the transit time of charge carriers through the depletion region.

LSA diode (Limited Space-charge Accumulation diode)
A microwave diode similar to the Gunn diode except that it achieves higher output power at frequencies, determined by the microwave cavity, that are several times greater than the transit-time frequency by avoiding the formation of charge bunches or domains.

Matched pair
A pair of diodes identical in outline dimensions and with matched electrical characteristics. The two diodes may both be forward polarity, or one forward and one reverse polarity, or both reverse polarity.

Microwave diode
A two terminal device that is responsive in the microwave region of the electro-magnetic spectrum, commonly extending from 1 to 300 GHz.

Mixer diode
A microwave diode that combines RF signals at two frequencies to generate an RF signal at a third frequency.

TRAPATT diode (TRApped Plasma Avalanche Transit Time diode)
A microwave diode that, when its junction is biased into avalanche, exhibits a negative resistance at frequencies below the transit time frequency range of the diode due to generation and dissipation of trapped electron-hole plasma resulting from the intimate interaction between the diode and a multi-resonant microwave cavity.

Microwave diode symbols

F_O	Overall average noise figure (of a mixer diode)
F_{OS}	Standard overall average noise figure (of a mixer diode)
L_C	Conversion loss
M	Figure of merit (of a detector diode)
N_r	Output noise ratio
TSS	Tangential signal sensitivity
VSWR	Voltage standing wave ratio
z_{if}	Impedance, intermediate-frequency
z_{rf}	Impedance, radio-frequency
z_m	Impedance, modulator-frequency load
z_v	Video impedance

Tunnel diodes

Backward diode

A device in which quantum-mechanical tunneling leads to a current-voltage characteristic with a reverse current greater than the forward current, for equal and opposite applied voltages. Quantum mechanics is a general mathematical theory dealing with the interactions of matter and radiation in terms of only observable quantities.

Tunnel diodes

A device in which quantum-mechanical tunneling leads to a region of negative slope in the forward direction of the current-voltage characteristic.

Tunnel diode and backward diode symbols

I_I .... Inflection point current

I_P .... Peak point current

I_V .... Valley point current

r_i .... Dynamic resistance at inflection point

V_{PP} .... Projected peak point voltage

V_I .... Inflection point voltage

V_P .... Peak point voltage

V_V .... Valley point voltage

Transient Voltage Suppressors (TVS) definitions

Avalanche junction
A transient voltage suppressor that is a semiconductor diode that can operate in either the forward or reverse direction of its voltage-current characteristic to limit voltage transients.

Clamping voltage
The voltage in a region of low differential resistance that serves to limit the transient voltage across the device terminals.

Clamping factor
The ratio of clamping voltage to breakdown voltage.

Forward surge current
The peak current for a single impulse for forward-biased diode.

Peak impulse current
The peak current for a series of essentially identical impulses.

Repetitive peak pulse power
The peak power dissipation resulting from the peak impulse current Ipp.

Response time
The time interval between the point on the impulse waveform at which the amplitude exceeds the clamping voltage level and the peak of the voltage overshoot.

Standby current
The DC current through a transient voltage suppressor at rated standoff voltage.

Varistor
A transient voltage suppressor that is a nonlinear resistor with symmetrical characteristics.

Voltage overshoot
The excess voltage over the clamping voltage that occurs when a current impulse having short virtual front duration is applied.

Working peak voltage
The peak voltage, excluding all transient voltage, usually referred to as standoff voltage.

Transient voltage suppressor symbols

CF .... Clamping factor

I_D .... Standby current

I_{FS} .... Forward surge current

I_{FSM} .... Rated forward surge current

I_{PP} .... Peak impulse current

I_{PPM} .... Rated peak impulse current

I_S .... Surge peak transient current

I_{SM} .... Rated surge peak transient current

$P_{(A)}$ .... Average power dissipation

$P_{M(A)}$ .... Rated average power dissipation

P_{PP} .... Repetitive peak pulse power dissipation

P_{PPM} .... Rated repetitive peak pulse power dissipation

t_{os} .... Overshoot duration

t_{res} .... Response time

$V_{(BR)}$ .... Breakdown voltage

V_C .... Clamping voltage

W_W .... Working peak voltage, also standoff voltage

$W_{WM(RMS)}$ .... Working rms voltage

V_{WM} .... Rated working peak voltage

V_{CS} .... Voltage overshoot

$\alpha V_{(BR)}$ .... Temperature coefficient of breakdown voltage

Varactor diode definitions

Tuning diode
A varactor diode used for RF tuning including functions such as automatic frequency control (AFC) and automatic fine tuning (AFT).

Varactor diode
A two terminal semiconductor device in which use is made of the property that its capacitance varies with the applied voltage.

Varactor diode symbols

C_C .... Case capacitance

C_j .... Junction capacitance

C_t .... Total capacitance

C_{t1} / C_{t2} .... Capacitance ratio

f_{co} .... Cut-off frequency

L_s .... Series inductance

Q .... Figure of merit

r_s .... resistance, small-signal

α_C .... Temperature coefficient of capacitance

η .... Efficiency

Thyristor definitions

Anode to cathode voltage-current characteristic (anode characteristic)
A function, usually represented graphically, relating the anode to cathode voltage to the principal current, with gate current where applicable, as a parameter.

Bidirectional diode thyristor
A two terminal thyristor having substantially the same switching behavior in the first and third quadrants of the principal voltage-current characteristic.

Bidirectional triode thyristor
An N-gate or P-gate thyristor having substantially the same switching behavior in the first and third quadrants of the principal voltage-current characteristic.

Breakover point
Any point on the principal voltage-current characteristic for which the differential resistance is zero and where the principal voltage reaches a maximum value.

Gate
An electrode connected to one of the semiconductor regions for introducing control current.

Main terminals
The two terminals through which the principal current flows.

N-gate thyristor
A three-terminal thyristor in which the gate terminal is connected to the N-region adjacent to the region to which the anode terminal is connected and that is normally switched to the ON-state by applying a negative signal between gate and anode terminals.

Negative differential resistance region
Any portion of the principal voltage-current characteristic in the switching quadrant within which the differential resistance is negative.

Off impedance
The differential impedance between the terminals through which the principal current flows when the thyristor is in the off-state.

Off-state
The condition of a thyristor corresponding to the high resistance low current portion of the principal voltage-current characteristic between the origin and the breakover point in the switching quadrant.

On impedance
The differential impedance between the terminals through which the principal current flows when the thyristor is in the on-state.

On-state
The condition of a thyristor corresponding to the low resistance, low voltage portion of the principal voltage-current characteristic in the switching quadrant.

P-gate thyristor
A three-terminal thyristor in which the gate terminal is connected to the p-region adjacent to the region to which the cathode terminal is connected and that is normally switched to the on-state by applying a positive signal between gate and cathode terminals.

Principal current
A generic term for the current through the device excluding gate current.

Principal voltage
The voltage between the main terminals.

Principal voltage-current characteristic (principal characteristic)
A function, usually represented graphically, relating the principal voltage to the principal current, with gate current where applicable, as a parameter.

Reverse blocking diode thyristor
A two-terminal thyristor that switches only for positive anode to cathode voltages and exhibits a reverse blocking state for negative anode to cathode voltages.

Reverse blocking impedance
The differential impedance between the two terminals through which the principal current flows when the thyristor is in the reverse blocking state at a stated operating point.

Reverse blocking state
The condition of a reverse blocking thyristor corresponding to the portion of the anode to cathode voltage-current characteristic for which the reverse currents are of lower magnitude than the reverse breakdown current.

Reverse blocking triode thyristor
An N-gate or P-gate thyristor that switches only for positive anode to cathode voltages and exhibits a reverse blocking state for negative anode to cathode voltages.

Reverse conducting diode thyristor
A two terminal thyristor that switches only for positive anode to cathode voltages and conducts large currents at negative anode to cathode voltages comparable in magnitude to the ON-state voltage.

Reverse conducting triode thyristor
An N-gate or P-gate thyristor that switches only for positive anode to cathode voltages and conducts large currents at negative anode to cathode voltages comparable in magnitude to the ON-state voltages.

Switching quadrant
A quadrant of the principal voltage-current characteristic in which a device is intended to switch between an OFF-state and an ON-state.

Thyristor
A bistable semiconductor device that comprises three or more junctions and can be switched between conducting (ON) and nonconducting (OFF) status.

Turn-off thyristor
A thyristor that can be switched between conducting and nonconducting states by applying control signals of appropriate polarities to the gate terminal, with the ratio of triggering power to triggered power appreciably less than one.

Thyristor symbols

dv/dt .... Crital rate of rise of off-state voltage

$I_{(BO)}$, $i_{(BO)}$ .... Breakover current

$I_{(BR)}$, $i_{(BR)}$ .... Reverse breakdown current (of a reverse-blocking thyristor)

$I_{D(RMS)}$, I_D, $I_{D(A)}$, i_D, I_{DM} .... Off-state current

I_{DRM} .... Repetitive peak off-state current

I_G, $I_{G(A)}$, i_G, I_{GM} .... Gate current

I_{GD}, i_{GD}, I_{GDM} .... Gate nontrigger current

I_{GQ}, i_{GQ}, I_{GQM} .... Gate turn-off current (of a turn-off thyristor)

I_{GT}, i_{GT}, I_{GTM} .... Gate trigger current

I_H, i_H .... Holding current

I_L, i_L .... Latching current

$I_{R(RSM)}$, I_R, $I_{R(A)}$, i_R, I_{RM} .... Reverse current (of a reverse-blocking or reverse-conducting thyristor)

I_{RRM} .... Repetitive peak reverse current (of a reverse-blocking thyristor)

I_{RSM} .... Nonrepetitive peak reverse current (of a reverse-blocking thyristor)

$I_{T(RMS)}$, I_T, $I_{T(A)}$, i_T, I_{TM} .... On-state current

I_{TRM} .... Repetitive peak on-state current

I_{TSM} .... Nonrepetitive peak on-state current

P_G, $P_{G(A)}$, P_G, P_{GM} .... Gate power dissipation

P_R, $P_{R(A)}$, P_R, P_{RM} .... Reverse power dissipation

t_{gd} .... Gate-controlled delay time

t_{gq} .... Gate-controlled turn-off time (of a turn-off thyristor)

t_{gt} .... Gate-controlled turn-on time

t_q .... Circuit-commutated turn-off time

$V_{(BO)}$, $v_{(BO)}$ .... Breakover voltage

$V_{(BR)}$, $v_{(BR)}$ .... Reverse breakdown voltage (of a reverse-blocking thyristor)

$V_{D(RMS)}$, V_D, $V_{D(A)}$, v_D, V_{DM} . Off-state voltage

V_{DRM} .... Repetitive peak off-state voltage

V_{DSM} .... Nonrepetitive peak off-state voltage

V_{DWM} .... Working peak off-state voltage

V_G, $V_{G(A)}$, v_G, V_{GM} .... Gate voltage

V_{GD}, v_{GD}, V_{GDM} .... Gate nontrigger voltage

V_{GQ}, v_{GQ}, V_{GQM} .... Gate turn-off voltage (of a turn-off thyristor)

V_{GT}, v_{GT}, V_{GTM} .... Gate trigger voltage (of a reverse-blocking thyristor

V_{RRM} .... Repetitive peak reverse voltage (of a reverse-blocking thyristor)

V_{RSM} .... Nonrepetitive peak reverse voltage (of a reverse-blocking thyristor)

V_{RWM} .... Working peak reverse voltage (of a reverse-blocking thyristor)

$V_{T(RMS)}$, V_T, $V_{T(A)}$, v_T, V_{TM} ... On-state voltage

$V_{T(MIN)}$ .... Minimum on-state voltage

LETTER SYMBOL TABLE FOR THYRISTORS.

	Total RMS value	DC value NO alternating component	DC value WITH alternating component	Instantaneous total value	Maximum (peak) total value
On-state current	$I_{T(RMS)}$	I_T	$I_{T(A)}$	i_T	I_{TM}
Repetitive peak, on-state current					I_{TRM}
Surge (nonrepetitive) on-state current				I_{TSM}	
Overload on-state current					$I_{T(OV)}$
Breakover current		$I_{(BO)}$		$i_{(BO)}$	
Off-state current	$I_{D(RMS)}$	I_D	$I_{D(A)}$	i_D	I_{DM}
Repetitive peak, off-state current					I_{DRM}
Reverse current	$I_{R(RMS)}$	I_R	$I_{R(A)}$	i_R	I_{RM}
Repetitive peak, reverse current					I_{RRM}
Reverse breakdown current		$I_{(BR)R}$		$i_{(BR)R}$	
On-state voltage	$V_{T(RMS)}$	V_T	$V_{T(A)}$	v_T	V_{TM}
Breakover voltage		$V_{(BO)}$		$v_{(BO)}$	
Off-state voltage	$V_{D(RMS)}$	V_D	$V_{D(A)}$	v_D	V_{DM}

	Total RMS value	DC value NO alternating component	DC value WITH alternating component	Instantaneous total value	Maximum (peak) total value
Minimum on-state voltage		$V_{T(MIN)}$			
Working peak, off-state voltage					V_{DWM}
Repetitive peak, off-state voltage					V_{DRM}
Nonrepetitive off-state voltage					V_{DSM}
Reverse voltage	$V_{R(RMS)}$	V_R	$V_{R(A)}$	v_R	V_{RM}
Working peak reverse voltage					V_{RWM}
Repetitive peak reverse voltage					V_{RRM}
Nonrepetitive peak, reverse voltage					V_{RSM}
Reverse breakdown voltage		$V_{(BR)R}$		$v_{(BR)R}$	
Holding current		I_H		i_H	
Latching current		I_L		i_L	
Gate current		I_G	$I_{G(A)}$	i_G	I_{GM}

	Total RMS value	DC value NO alternating component	DC value WITH alternating component	Instantaneous total value	Maximum (peak) total value
Gate trigger current		I_{GT}		i_{GT}	I_{GTM}
Gate nontrigger current		I_{GD}		i_{GD}	I_{GDM}
Gate turn-off current		I_{GQ}		i_{GQ}	I_{GQM}
Gate voltage		V_G	$V_{G(A)}$	v_G	V_{GM}
Gate trigger voltage		V_{GT}		v_{GT}	V_{GTM}
Gate nontrigger current		V_{GD}		v_{GD}	V_{GDM}
Gate turn-off voltage		V_{GQ}		v_{GQ}	V_{GQM}
Gate power dissipation		P_G	$P_{G(A)}$	P_G	P_{GM}

Light Emitting Diode (LED) definitions

Backlighting
Illumination by an indicator of a front panel legend from behind, without protrusion of the LED through the panel.

Bicolor LED
A component that contains two LED dice of different colors in a single substrate or lead-frame carrier. The components have either two, three (common cathode), or four lead wires for turning the devices ON and OFF.

Candela (cd)
The standard unit measure of luminous intensity which is used to calculate lumen and foot candle measurements.

Continuous forward current
The current that must be applied to the P-side of an optoelectronic device such as an LED to produce a given output.

Crosslalk (light bleed)
The undesired illumination of one indicator position by the light source trom another.

Current-limiting resistor
A protective resistor added in-line between the power source and the light source to regulate current delivered to the device. The value of the resistor depends on the operating voltage of the circuit.

Diagnostic application
One of two applications served by circuit board indicators (the other being front panel applications). In diagnostic applications. the indicator is mounted on a circuit board, generally without secondary optics, and is viewed at close range by a service technician inside a piece of equipment.

Die
The basic semiconductor device or "chip" inside the LED assembly.

Diffusant
Glass particles suspended in the epoxy lens of an LED that diffuse the light and broaden the device's viewing angle.

Direct view

The application of an indicator in which its lens protrudes through the front panel and is viewed directly.

Dominant wavelength

The wavelength at which the human eye perceives light emitted from an LED to be strongest.

Electroluminescence

The nonthermal conversion of electrical energy into light. In an LED. it is produced by electron-hole recombination in the PN junction.

Epoxy

A resin characterized by high adhesiveness, toughness. and corrosion resistance Used to surround LED die to provide atributes such as diffusion and lens shape.

Foot-candle

A unit for measuring illumination. One foot-candle equals the amount of light delivered by a 1-candela light source to a 1sq. ft. surface, 1 ft. away.

Front panel application

The application of an LED in which the light is viewed at the front panel of the host equipment This usually requires either backlighting or direct-view configuration.

Forward voltage

The voltage that must be applied to the P-side of an optoelectronic device such as an LED to produce a given output.

Integral resistor

An LED design option in which the current-limiting resistor is contained within the package.

Infrared

The region of the electromagnetic spectrum between the long wavelength extreme of the visible spectrum (700 nm) and the shortest microwave frequencies (10^7nm or 1mm). Nearly all of the infrared portion of the spectrum is invisible to the human eye. Infrared LEDs are used in sensing, data transmission, ambient light defection, and other various applications.

Lead frame

A metal structure to which a semiconductor die is attached. The lead frame provides stability for the devices and completes the electrical path to the die.

Lens

The epoxy enclosure molded to an LED die to provide optical characteristics.

Light Emitting Diode (LED)

A PN junction semiconductor device that emits incoherent, monochromatic, optical radiation when biased in the forward direction.

Light pipe

An optical conduit made of molded plastic that directs the light from an LED to the viewing location, often at a right angle from the circuit board.

Lumen

A unit of luminous flux equal to the luminous flux emitted by a standard point source having a luminous intensity of one candela.

Millicandela (mcd)

One thousandth of a candela.

Nanometer (nm)

One billionth of 1 meter. Often used (along with angstroms) to quantify the wavelength of light.

Neon lamp

A light source that generates a blue or amber light by exciting a neon gas plasma with healed electrodes.

Operating current

The current which a device such as an LED is designed to draw from the power source.

Operating temperature

The range of temperature over which a device will safely operate.

Operating voltage
The voltage or range of voltages al which a device is designed to operate.

PN junction
Holes and electrons combine in the negative (N) region of a positive-negative (PN) junction semiconductor diode During these shifts in energy, photons are generated, some of which are absorbed by the semiconductor material and some of which are emitted as light energy.

Power dissipation
The amount of power dissipated as heat by a device.

Prism
A device used to separate a light beam into its spectral components. A prism could be used to direct light output from an LED to the viewing location.

Reflector cup
A coined portion of a lead frame that forms a reflector around the periphery of an LED die and directs its light output. The reflector cup is an integral part of the device and is unique to the lead-frame type rather than substrate-type chip carrier.

Right-angle viewing
A type of indicator application in which the light output must be viewed at a right angle (i.e., in a direction parallel to the circuit board).

Reverse breakdown voltage
The reverse voltage applied to a diode, which if exceed, will cause the device to fail. Specifically, the value when a diode is reversed biased that avalanche breakdown occurs.

Secondary optics
Devices that are used to enhance or redirect the light output of an LED. Examples include lenses and light pipes.

Super-bright LED
An LED designed to produce exceptionally high light intensity.

SMD
Acronym for Surface-Mount Device.

SMT
Acronym for Surface-Mount Technology.

Surface-mount LED
LED designed to conform to the requirements of the surface mount circuit-board manufacturing environment Surface mount devices must withstand the soldering process and must be physically compatible with automated pick-and-place equipment.

Through-hole LED
The most common type of LED package it is connected to the circuit board via its leads that also serve as the interface to the power source. The through-hole LED is not surface mountable.

Tint
A color added to the epoxy lens of an LED to identify its color when "ON."

Transparent substrate
A characteristic of an LED die which increases its light output. The substrate on which the upper portion of the die is grown is a transparent semiconductor material that does not absorb the light energy.

Tricolor LED
A component that contains two LED dice of different colors in a single substrate or lead-frame carrier. The components have either two. three (common cathode), or four leads for turning the devices ON and OFF. This LED can a so be called a bicolor LED.

Viewing angle
The area in front and to the sides of an LED at which light output falls to 50 percent. The viewable area appears as a cone-shaped pattern.

Visible spectrum
The light spectrum between 400 and 700 nm which is detectable by the human eye.

Water clear LED
An LED die combined with a clear lens that has no tinting is sometimes refered to as a water clear LED.

Optoelectronic device definitions

Conversion efficiency
The ratio of maximum available power output resulting from photovoltaic operation to total incident radiant flux.

Dark condition
The condition attained when the electrical parameter under consideration approaches a value which cannot be altered by further irradiation shielding.

Dark current
The current that flows through a photosensitive device in the dark condition.

Light current
The current that flows through a photosensitive device when it is exposed to radiant energy.

Optoelectronic device
A device that is responsive to or that emits or modifies electromagnetic radiation in the visible, infrared, or ultraviolet spectral regions; or a device that utilizes such electromagnetic radiation for its internal operation.

Photoconductive diode
A photodiode that is intended to be used as a photoconductive transducer.

Photocurrent
The difference in magnitude between light current and dark current.

Photodiode
A diode that is intended to be responsive to radiant energy.

Photodiode, avalanche
A photodiode that is intended to take advantage of avalanche multiplication of photocurrent.

Photoemitter
A device that emits electromagnetic radiation in the visible, infrared, or ultraviolet spectral regions.

Photosensitive device

A device that is responsive to electromagnetic radiation in the visible, infrared, or ultraviolet spectral regions.

Photothyristor

A thyristor that is intended to be responsive to radiant energy for controlling its operation as a thyristor.

Phototransistor

A transistor that is intended to be responsive to radiant energy.

Photovoltaic diode

A photodiode that is intended to generate a terminal voltage in response to radiant energy.

Optoelectronic device symbols

$Q, (Q_e)$ .... Radiant energy

$Q, (Q_v)$ .... Luminous energy

t_d .... Delay time

t_f .... Fall time

t_{off} .... Turn-off time

t_{on} .... Turn-on time

t_r .... Rise time

t_s .... Storage time

t .... Time constant

f .... Luminous flux, radiant flux

Optocoupler device definitions

Photodarlington coupler
An optocoupler in which the photosensitive element is a Darlington connected phototransistor.

Photodiode coupler
An optocoupler in which the photosensitive element is a photodiode.

Photothyristor coupler
An optocoupler in which the photosensitive element is a photothyristor.

Phototransistor coupler
An optocoupler in which the photosensitive element is a phototransistor.

Optocoupler (photocoupler and optoisolator) symbols

C_{io} .... Input-to-output internal capacitance; transcapacitance

h_F .... Current transfer ratio

I_{IO} .... DC input-to-output current; isolation current

r_{IO} .... Isolation resistance

V_{IO} .... DC input-to-output voltage; isolation voltage

Photoemitting device definitions

Avalanche luminescent diode
A light emitting diode that emits luminous energy when a controlled reverse current in the breakdown region is applied.

Infrared emitting diode
A diode capable of emitting radiant energy in the infrared region of the spectrum resulting from the recombination of electrons and holes.

Light emitting diode (LED)
A diode capable of emitting luminous energy resulting from the recombination of electrons and holes.

Radiant efficiency
The ratio of the total radiant flux emitted to the total input power.

Photoemitting device symbols

I	Luminous intensity; radiant intensity
L	Luminance; radiance
tf	Radiant-pulse fall time
tr	Radiant-pulse rise time
w	Lumininous density; radiant density
Δl	Spectral bandwidth
λ_p	Peak wavelength

Photosensitive device symbols

A_D .... Area, detector

E .... Illuminance (illumination); irradiance

f_{mod} .... Modulation frequency

I_n .... Detector noise

I_S, I_s .... signal current (DC; rms value of AC component)

P_n .... Noise equivalent power

V_n .... Detector noise voltage

V_S, V_s .... signal voltage (DC; rms value of AC component)

μf .... Noise equivalent bandwidth

Bibliography

Many thanks to the following who gave permission to use their information for reference or for incorporation into this book:

Dialight Corp., Manasquan, NJ 08736: *Circuit Board Indicators Technical Data Book* (96 Edition).

General Semiconductor, Inc., Melville, NY 11747: *Small Signal Transistors, Schottky Diodes an·' Switching Diodes* Databook *(9/98). Power Rectifiers & Transient Vo. .ge Suppressors* Databook (5/98).

Rohm Electronics U.S.A, Antioch, TN 37013: *Opto Devices, '97 - '98, DataBook.*

Vishay Intertechnology, Inc. Malvern, PA 19355
Vishay Telefunken (formerly Temic) *Diodes Data Book* 1996.
Small-Signal Discrete Products 1997.

Voltage Multipliers, Inc., Visalia, CA 93291: *VMI Data Book*, (3rd Edition)

Additional Refer nces:

American Microsemiconductor Inc., Madison, NJ

D.O.D MIL-PRF-19500L, *Performance Specification Semiconductor Devices, General Specification For,* 22 October 1998.

Appendix A

High-End Audio Applications

High-end audio is one of the few subjective areas of electronic design. In almost all fields of hardware development a system either works or it does not. In high-end audio component design, it is entirely possible to have a piece of equipment that works (meets all paper specifications) and sounds horrible.

Component selection in areas that would appear to be insignificant to the success of a design can effect the ultimate sound quality of a component in a negative way. One of the areas that is overlooked is the input rectifier that lives off the secondary of the power transformer. Traditionally, the rectifiers were standard recovery diodes. On the surface this would appear to be a good selection, since the fundamental frequency of the line current is 60Hz (50Hz in Europe).

Critical listening ests have demonstrated that the recovery time and type (soft or snappy) has an effect on the "subjective quietness" of a high-end audio product. This is not "quietness" from the standpoint of signal-to-noise ratio traditionally measured in decibels. This is a subjective sense of silence between notes in a musical passage. To investigate further, this phenomenon can be measured with a spectrum analyzer. The higher order harmonics generated by the recovery time of the standard speed rectifier can be clearly viewed on the spectrum analyzer. These upper harmonics are absent or at least below the noise floor of the instrumentation. Audiophiles spend lots of money on AC line conditioners to eliminate line noise from the power supply inputs to their equipment, which is certainly counter productive to generating this noise internally. This component substitution is easy to accomplish.

Power amplifiers typically use a bridge rectifier after the power transformer. When bridges are not used, it is necessary to build the bridge assembly out of components utilizing the speed and recovery waveform of Schottky rectifiers.

In low-voltage applications, many solid state designs can utilize Schottky rectifiers. Schottky rectifiers have switching speeds in the single nanosecond times and below. These are ideal for almost all solid state preamplifiers, CD players, digital processors, tuners, high-end surround sound, low-voltage class "A" power amps and tube filament supplies.

Tubes (also known as valves) are still widely used in high-end audio circuitry. These components require much higher operating voltages than solid state designs. Schottky rectifiers are ideal for tube preampliers and for valve power amplifiers.

Attention to the front end of the power supply in high-grade audio gear is essential, if a design is going to deliver the best possible sound quality. In addition, it is possible to design "AC line conditioning" into the AC front end of the power supply, minimizing the need for external power conditioning equipment. When all this is done, the DC rails of properly designed equipment should be unbelievably quiet.

Appendix B

Equations

Metric Prefixes

Pico	x 10^{-12}		Tera	x 10^{12}
Nano	x 10^{-9}		Giga	x 10^{9}
Micro	x 10^{-6}		Mega	x 10^{6}
Milli	x 10^{-3}		Kilo	x 10^{3}
Deci	x 10^{-1}		Deca	x 10^{1}

Symbols

E = Voltage in *Volts* C = Capacitance in *Farads*

I = Current in *Amperes* L = Inductance in *Henries*

R = Resistance in *Ohms* X_C = Capacitive Reactance in *Ohms*

P = Power in *Watts* X_L = Inductive Reactance in *Ohms*

Basic Formulas

1. Ohm's Law

$$E = IR = \frac{P}{I} = \sqrt{PR} \qquad I = \frac{E}{R} = \frac{P}{E} = \sqrt{\frac{P}{R}}$$

$$R = \frac{E}{I} = \frac{E^2}{P} = \frac{P}{I^2} \qquad P = I^2R = \frac{E^2}{R} = EI$$

2. Resistance in Series
$$R_T = R_1 + R_2 + R_3 + R_4 + ...$$

3. Resistance in Parallel
$$\frac{1}{R_T} = \frac{1}{R_1} + \frac{1}{R_2} + \frac{1}{R_3} + ...$$

$$R_T = \frac{R_1 \times R_2}{R_1 + R_2} \quad (For\, 2\, Resistors\, Only)$$

$$R_T = \frac{R_1}{\#\ of\ Resistors} \quad (For\ Equal\, Resistors)$$

4. Capacitance in Series
Computed like resistance in Parallel.

5. Capacitance in Parallel
Computed like resistance in Series.

6. Inductance in Series
Computed like resistance in Series.

7. Inductance in Parallel
Computed like resistance in Parallel.

8. Capacitive Reactance8

$$X_C = \frac{1}{2\,\pi\,f\,C} \quad (f = Frequency\ in\ Hz)$$

9. Inductive Reactance
$$X_L = 2\,\pi\,f\,L \quad (f = Frequency\ in\ Hz)$$

10. Noise Index
$$db = 20 \times \log_{10} \frac{Noise\ Voltage\,(over\, a\ 1\ decade\ bandwith)}{DC\ Voltage}$$

11. Parts Per Million (ppm): Conversion of % to ppm

%	ppm	%	ppm
0.0001%	1	0.01%	100
0.0002%	2	0.02%	200
0.0005%	5	0.025%	250
0.001%	10	0.05%	500
0.0025%	25	0.1%	1,000
0.005%	50	1.0%	10,000

Formula is: $\dfrac{0.0001\% \times 10^6}{100} = 1\ ppm$

12. Frequency (f)

$$f = \frac{1}{2\pi \sqrt{LC}}$$

NOTES:

Index

Notes

Printed in Great Britain
by Amazon.co.uk, Ltd.,
Marston Gate.